Paupers Progress

From Poor Relief to an Old Age Pension

a short history
by

Joe Harris

Foreword

It is a privilege to be asked to contribute these few words to Joe Harris' short book because, although it has been very carefully researched and would grace the shelves of any university library, it is part of a very special British heritage, the people's history. *Paupers' Progress*, like Dave Goodman's *No Thanks to Lloyd George*, provides a perspective on old age that is rooted in the pensioners' movement and the daily struggle for a decent pension. If scientists contribute at all to this campaign (and most do not), we are very rarely involved closely as participants like Joe Harris and his colleagues in the National Pensioners Convention. Thus, the analyses in this booklet are underpinned by a commitment to social justice and anger that the needs of Britain's older people have not been recognised fully, especially in the form of a decent income available to all of them regardless of employment history. *Paupers' Progress* charts the exclusion and degradation of older people over the last seven centuries and, in doing so, exposes the roots of the present paternalistic and demeaning attitudes towards older people and the inadequacies of public pensions. The case for public risk pooling for old age was made in Britain as early as the thirteenth century and periodically reiterated over the years. As Joe Harris shows, older people were identified as the 'deserving poor' in the nineteenth century, partly due to the work of Charles Booth, and then ensued the long campaign for a decent pension. The first major success was the 1908 old age pension, though 'old age' began at 70 and, given the low level of the pension and the continuance of poverty into old age, the campaign continued and, indeed, still does today.

Although this is an historical account, it has crystal clear relevance for the pensions debate taking place today in the wake of the reports from the Pensions Commission. While destitution in old age is rare in modern Britain; as Joe Harris argues, there are still an unacceptably large number of older people living in poverty and being excluded from mainstream society. Older people are still dying prematurely, including several thousand every winter as a result of cold, or living with disabilities following strokes or other avoidable tragedies. Too often still, in twenty-first century Britain, provision for older people is discussed in terms of 'benevolence' or 'deservingness' rather than human and social rights.

Joe Harris argues that what is required to achieve the goal that campaigners have fought to realise for more than a century – the abolition of poverty in old age – is the remarkably modest sum of £150 per week. However, the only way that such a sum could be delivered immediately, guaranteed in perpetuity and inflation proofed is by government action using collective contributions and/or taxes. British society, collectively, has achieved a massive social advance in enabling millions of older people to reach old age, an experience that very few underwent in previous generations. What is needed now is a similar collective endeavour to enable *all* of them to live in dignity. Joe Harris' voice, speaking for the five million older people either living in poverty or on its margins and the countless millions of future pensioners who face similar insecurity, deserves the widest possible audience and demands an answer from policy makers.

Alan Walker,
Professor of Social Policy and Social Gerontology, University of Sheffield
Patron, National Pensioners Convention

Contents

Introduction

Introduction

Before the 1908 old age pension, almost everyone was dependent upon family or charity for food and shelter in their old age. In medieval times the principal provider of charity was the church, but in the sixteenth century this was seriously affected by the dissolution of the monasteries. People in extreme poverty could no longer rely upon church help for survival, and growing urbanisation and the weakening of medieval settled family life exacerbated the situation, especially for the old and frail. To maintain civic stability, Elizabethan England encouraged the parishes to take on increased responsibilities for maintaining their poor, and in the latter years of the century this responsibility was made mandatory. In 1601, significant state involvement in the provision of poor relief was consolidated in the Poor Law of Elizabeth I. The funding required was raised by a poor rate levied on better-off residents.

The resultant parish support was hardly generous. Barely enough for survival, it was available only to those unable to work and care for themselves, and if they 'deserved it'. It was a last resort. Large numbers of older people relied upon the food the parish could provide, sheltered in the poorhouse and, later on, in the workhouse. They were paupers.

Since Elizabethan times we have made great strides in raising the average standard of living. In modern industrial Britain, we no longer talk of 'paupers' or see people dying of starvation in the street. Indeed, some people manage to put a bit under the mattress or take out private pensions and look forward to retiring on a good income. However, not everyone is able to save for their old age – most rely upon state or occupational pensions. Those who are lucky enough to receive occupational pensions find that because they depend upon past earnings, which were much less than those prevailing today, they seldom provide for the hoped-for lifestyle. The full basic state retirement pension is less than Income Support and millions of pensioners live below the official poverty line. They are subjected to a means-test to make ends meet in order to obtain state handouts on which they depend.

In spite of all the progress, 'If you're old, it's on the cards you will be poor.' But, it's no longer acceptable that 'economically inactive' older citizens, any more than children, should live below the poverty line, or that a charitable handout or two are all that is needed to alleviate their immediate suffering. In the following pages I outline the progress Britain has made over the centuries in defeating old age destitution and poverty. What has been achieved is not primarily due to enlightenment or moral progress. It has depended upon the growth in national wealth that has taken place over the years, and the valiant efforts of many good men and women in overcoming resistance to transferring part of it to those in need. The arguments they encountered against doing so are much the same as those advanced today. Moreover, the imposition of demeaning conditions and the patronising attitudes that accompanied so much of the attempts to provide for the poor, are still to be seen in present-day approaches to improve the quality of life for the older generation.

On the parish
'Those were the days!'

The fourteenth century saw a quarter of Europe's population being claimed by the Black Death and the breakdown of the feudal manorial system. Barely existing on their low wages, peasants throughout Europe demanded more and rebelled. In England, the imposition of a poll tax sparked off the Peasants' Revolt which all but overturned the king and ruling landowners. While there was plenty of work to do, there was a dramatic shortage of labour and it was in the interests of landowners to ensure the full employment of all available fit persons in their locality, so in 1349, Edward III decreed a 'Statute of Labourers'. This laid down that 'every able-bodied man and woman of the realm ... within the age of three score years ... unless in commerce, crafts or with independent means ... be required to work ... if not ... to be taken and committed to gaol and held until he finds surety to serve'. Poverty of the able-bodied was associated with work avoidance, so the law stated that 'None, on the pain of imprisonment, shall give alms to a beggar capable of labour'. In other words if you were able and didn't work then you couldn't count on any assistance – indeed, you could expect harsh treatment. Applied to the fit and active, this attitude was not altogether unreasonable when there was plenty of work available. But it was a bit hard on the old and weak.

If you were quite unable to work the parish was expected to take on a responsibility for your maintenance. In order to make this system of relief function, the destitute were required to remain in their parish. In 1376, with the aim of reducing the number of urban vagrants, it was decreed that 'idlers' without residential rights should be banished from cities and towns or imprisoned. Furthermore, to discourage begging, in his Act XII of 1388, Richard II laid down that 'beggars impotent to serve' were not to travel from the village or town in which they resided but must remain in the parish of their abode so as to be assisted. If they could not be maintained there, they were to be sent back to the parish of their birth.

By 1514 the only beggars allowed in York and London were the 'deserving poor' who had been granted a *licence*. In 1524 a statute by Henry VIII ruled that licences and badges were to be granted only to the 'impotent', 'aged' and 'feeble' who could not earn their living through labour and to nobody else. (These badges were not dispensed with until 1834 when the new Poor Law was introduced).[1] Effectively, begging was outlawed. It was prohibited to give alms to able-bodied unlicensed beggars. If a person was caught by the local authority giving alms to a beggar, they suffered a penalty of a fine of up to ten times the amount given.

Poverty equated to destitution level, so identification of who was poor was a simple straightforward task: no means-test was necessary. The important decision of whether the poor person was 'deserving' was however not so clear, and judgement on whether he or she was 'impotent' to do some work would depend upon an estimation of capability at that particular time. Whilst this was easily assessed in the case of physical disability, it may not have been so clear in cases of some poor souls afflicted with illness or disease.

This law did not, of course, stop good people sheltering and helping those in extreme poverty. Indeed, it was customary for rich people to will part of their estates to help the poor and many established 'almshouses' to shelter them. Since before the ninth century, almshouses had been established by religious orders and attached to abbeys and monasteries. Those endowed through legacies of wealthy benefactors were usually intended to house and sustain a specified grouping of elderly and needy people defined by the benefactor, for example, residents of a particular locality or aged and retired workers of a particular trade.

[1] Wilfred A. Sealey, 'Ulster beggars' badges', *Ulster Journal of Archaeology*, **33**, 1970.

The oldest almshouse still operating is The Hospital of St Cross which can be found in Winchester. Now modernised and with central heating, it was founded in 1136 by Henry de Blois, Bishop of Winchester to house 13 'poor men'. Mary Westbury's Almshouse in Hoxton Causey, London (set up in 1749) was originally for 'poor widows' and 'Protestant Dissenters professing Presbyterian, Independent or Antipaedobaptist tenets'. They received pensions of three shillings (later four shillings) per week plus a 'chaldron of coal' (18 cwts)[2]. Almshouses were had their own rules. For instance, one almshouse, St Mary Magdalene's Hospital in Kings Lynn, which was founded in 1146 stipulated that anyone caught wearing low shoes instead of regulation high boots was made to walk barefoot for a season.

In the sixteenth century, the Enclosure Act of 1538 enabled the rich to take over great swathes of common land. This resulted in the uprooting of many families and increased the numbers of vagrants and the destitute of all ages. It was very difficult to avoid destitution if you were old, and old people made up a large proportion of these unfortunates out of proportion to the numbers of the aged in the total population. Hardly any old people had savings and many were alone, having no one to support them. For example, a census of the poor taken in Ipswich parishes in 1597 showed that in the three largest parishes, 54 (39 per cent) out of the 140 poor receiving outdoor relief were 60 and over. Over all the nine parishes where relief was recorded, 33 per cent of recipients were aged 60 and over – many times more than their percentage of the adult population at that time.[3]

The increasing concentration of wealth in the sixteenth century financed trading activity in Europe and laid the basis for the Industrial Revolution. It also meant that social structures of town and country began to alter. Existing charities and almshouses could not cope with the increasing numbers of poor and aged paupers.

England was not alone in having to deal with the social problems created by the growth of trade, manufacturing and urbanisation. Venice was

---

[2] Today, some 26,000 separate almshouses, mostly founded in the nineteenth century, accommodate some 40,000 elderly people, representing a capital cost saving to the state of between £2 and 3 billion and an annual revenue cost of around £500 million.

[3] J.F. Pound, 'An Elizabethan census of the poor', *University of Birmingham Historical Journal*, 8(2), 1962.

developing its own merchant capitalism at about the same time and experiencing a similar increase in the numbers of its poor. Like London and other English urban centres, prosperous Venice had attracted the rural poor and destitute in search of work and sustenance. In an attempt to prevent the problem of dealing with this influx of impoverished people, in 1529 the Venetian senate decreed that the poor who entered their city from outside must be sent back to their own territories where the priests of their native parishes would have to provide for them.

As far as the indigenous poor were concerned, the senate ruled that the infirm were to receive charity in their particular parish, and the funds necessary were to be raised by the priest from his parishioners. Masters of Vessels lying in Venice and the fleet would be invited to take on able-bodied destitute men as sailors at half-pay. If this did not suffice to deal with the problem, then the craft brotherhoods should employ those remaining without work and provide for them 'according to their need and as they judge best'.[4] This was perhaps an early form of 'workfare' but it depended upon work being available and the willingness of the able pauper to accept work at low pay as better than resorting to crime to avoid starvation. The old who were unable to work were provided for by the parish.

In England, between 1536 and 1547, the dissolution of the monasteries reduced the availability of care for the poor and aged significantly. It became urgently necessary to strengthen and organise existing secular poor relief. In the twenty-seventh year of his reign Henry VIII brought in the English Beggars Act. Bearing some similarities to the Venetian rulings, the Act made individual parishes responsible for their poor and it also provided for local officers to supervise alms. The actual relief given to the poor varied from parish to parish, depending upon the discretion of the officers and the sums collected. Poverty was not evenly distributed and parish generosity was not uniform. In 1572, Elizabeth I improved the position by establishing these parish officers as 'Overseers of the Poor' (who came from amongst local substantial householders) and legislating to give them the right to levy compulsory poor rates.

Later Acts in 1597 and 1601 confirmed these earlier Acts and gave

[4] D. Chambers and B. Pullan (eds) with J. Fletcher, *Venice, A Documentary History 1450–1630*, Blackwell, Oxford, 1992.

additional powers to local overseers to arrange work, housing and sustenance for the parish poor. The 1601 'Acte for the Reliefe of the Poore' (43 Eliz. I c. ii), which was to become known as the 'Poor Law', and was to lay the basis of subsequent Poor Laws, ruled that a parish must provide for its poor, and house the homeless. This Act is very significant – it was the first step by the state, via its parishes, to take responsibility for its poor people. Because of it, the provision of relief was no longer seen as exclusively the preserve of voluntary charities. It had become a *duty of the state* and the *people's right*.

This legal obligation was made universal by the Act of 1622. Local overseers were responsible to justices who were empowered to make a special levy on adjoining parishes to supplement available funds where this was necessary. Costs were to be met by raising a local tax on landowners or tenants. Failure to pay could result in fines, seizure of property or imprisonment. The parish gentlemen, who had to provide the funds, paid a 'poor rate' to the overseers based upon the value of the property which they tenanted. Consequently, they continuously campaigned and contrived to keep the costs of relief as low as possible.

Like the Venetians, the better-off parishioners certainly didn't welcome the arrival of poor from other parishes. It was hardly a coincidence, therefore, that an Act to restrict the travel of the destitute followed in 1662. This 'Vagrancy Act' not only consolidated the existing laws but was also aimed at preventing the unauthorised movement of beggars and unemployed people by the imposition of harsh penalties. It stipulated that 'rogues, vagabonds and sturdy beggars', men and women, found outside their parish were to be 'stripped naked from the waist upward and openly whipped until his or her body be bloudye'. Charity was thus limited.

Following the end of the Commonwealth and the restoration of the monarchy, Charles II reinforced legislation that prevented unemployed labourers travelling in search of work. However, as there was a need at times for casual employment of labour from outside the parish, William III later introduced a kind of 'paupers' passport' to enable some, with permission, to travel. This pass law was to remain in force until 1795. Nonetheless, vagrancy continued to be unlawful and legislation defined the residential conditions to be met by a pauper to qualify for parish relief.

In the reign of George III, a metropolitan court warrant could be made out for the forcible removal of a pauper trespasser from a parish. In effect, the pauper could be treated as a criminal. This harsh treatment of the vagrant poor, including older men and women, remained the law until 1847.

In addition to excluding paupers from 'abroad', parishes were also wary of allowing anyone to settle in their area if the person was likely to become destitute. A right to 'settlement' was only granted automatically to those who themselves or whose parents were born in the parish. It could also be granted to those apprenticed there or to those paying rates or rent for lodgings of at least £10 per year (an agricultural worker's wage at that time was about £3 per year). All these conditions were clearly aimed at reducing the likelihood that the parish would become financially responsible for incomers.

The Act of 1622 had permitted churchwardens, with the support of two justices, to order new arrivals, during their first 40 days of residence, back to their last place of settlement if it was considered they were likely to become claimants for relief. Indeed, special officers were sometimes engaged to carry out the transportation of poor souls with no settlement rights back to the parish which was believed to be responsible for them. Old and young ordered back to their original parishes suffered great hardship. The law laid down that they had to travel at least 10 miles each day, in as a direct route as possible, towards their parish of settlement under pain of punishment. As many of these poor people were not only aged but destitute, frail, hungry and cold, this must have been a cruel ordeal.

Removing the poor from one parish to another became a profitable occupation. As late as 1834 a man of 90 was sent from Bristol back to the parish of Steyning in Sussex during midwinter. Instead of making him walk there, Bristol 'humanely' arranged for him to travel by coach – no doubt influenced by the fact that the costs of his return, including that of the officer accompanying him, and the coach fare, had to be paid for, not by Bristol but by his settlement parish of Steyning. He was bundled onto a coach with 'neither rug nor coat to cover him'. His experience was recorded because, when he had to change coaches in London, he was so obviously ill that he was taken to St Bartholomew's Hospital. The doctors there, not surprisingly, stated that for him to continue his journey would have been fatal. His final fate is not recorded.

A large number of the poor wandering around England in the first half of the nineteenth century was Irish. Between 1841 and 1851 the population of Ireland had fallen from 9 million to 6.5 million as a result of a series of famines.[5] About 1,400,000 Irish men, women and children had starved to death; the rest had migrated. It is difficult to imagine the scale of suffering of the Irish people. Even after the end of the 'Great Famine' in 1847 old and young alike were still starving, and typhus, scurvy and cholera continued to wreak havoc, even in areas that had escaped the worst of previous years. Indeed, one reason for the vigorous application of the English settlement regulations may have been a fear that an increasing number of poor Irish would come to seek work in England in order to send money home to keep their old parents, wives and children alive.

During the latter half of the nineteenth century the conditions for settlement were progressively relaxed, mainly to ensure mobility of labour. With the onset of the Industrial Revolution, this was becoming essential for rapidly growing industry. Nevertheless, the expulsion of the poor who were unable to claim settlement from the parish in which they had become destitute continued. As late as 1907 more than 12,000 poor people were 'removed' from parishes. Perhaps the rules of settlement gave rise to the saying 'Charity begins at home'. It certainly wasn't thriving elsewhere.

In addition to the parish's 'problem' of dealing with the arrival of an adult vagrant was that presented by the inconsiderate birth of a baby born out of wedlock. The Act of 1610 (7, James I, c. v) had legislated that 'every lewde woman having a bastarde which may be chargeable to the parish' should be 'committed to a House of Correction to be punished and set to work for one year'. There was no mention of the father in the Act and it seems its most vital concern was to protect the parish from becoming in some way financially responsible for the poor child. An illegitimate child was not entitled to adopt the father's parish of settlement. If, as was so often the case, the baby needed poor relief for its survival, it became a charge on the parish where it was born. It was not

---

[5] Sir G. Nicholls, *The History of the Irish Poor Law*, John Murray, London, 1856.

until 1733 that a father could be gaoled if, having been identified and found, he refused to indemnify the parish against the cost of any relief provided to the child.

Therefore, the overseers made great efforts to 'remove' unmarried pregnant women. These unfortunate women were hardly the most able to suffer the trauma of banishment but then, historically, treatment of poor unmarried mothers-to-be has never been exactly humane.

Poor Laws were to remain in force until 1948. Whilst legislating for the sustaining of the poor, they aimed to minimise parochial expense in so doing. They laid great emphasis that those receiving help should be deserving and had, before claiming assistance, led moral and thrifty lives. It could be suggested that this view prevails today in attitudes to the the poor in need.

Workfare

The Elizabethans believed that the way to alleviate poverty was to put the poor to work. As this was not the first concern of landowners or tradesmen, some governmental intervention was necessary. As noted above, in 1597 parish overseers were appointed. In addition to other duties, they were also charged with apprenticing and setting to work children who couldn't be supported by their families. By this time, poorhouses had also been established wherein the destitute children could live with unemployed adults, including old people, who would also be provided with work.

One of the earliest poorhouses was opened in Ipswich in 1572. Endowed through a 1551 bequest of a wealthy merchant Henry Tooley, its aim was to cope with two classes of the poor: firstly, the aged, orphans, widows, the sick and others in want and secondly, vagrants and vagabonds who were begging 'without real necessity'. Inmates were clothed and fed and each received a cash allowance directly from collections. The aged, young and sick were looked after by a 'guider', who, in addition to holding and administering funds, also organised a programme of work for the able, and purchased the necessary materials. The main activities were carding and spinning but it is recorded that there was a brief participation in a municipal candle-making factory. The regime was generally humanitarian. A local haven was provided for old poor people. In 1579 there were about 36 inmates.[6]

The first state initiative to deal with homeless people was taken by Elizabeth I. Under an Act in 1590 it had become illegal, excepting in special cases, such as for housing quarry workers, etc. to build a house or

---

[6] J. Webb, *Poor Relief in Elizabethan Ipswich*, Suffolk Records Society, **9**, 1966.

cottage on a piece of land smaller than four acres. It was also against the law to house more than one family in a single cottage. By the thirty-ninth year of her reign (1597/8), the numbers of the destitute and vagrants had increased so much as to make it necessary to pass an Act to set up special houses for the poor. These were to accommodate 'the lame, impotente olde, blinde and suche other ... being poore and unable to work'. The Act commanded that parishes should appoint, from amongst substantial householders, an Overseer of the Poor to work closely with the churchwardens in establishing and administrating these poorhouses. The houses or cottages would be built on waste land with the agreement of the lord of the manor. More than one person or family could be housed in each.

These 'Howses of Dwellinge for the saide impotente poore' were the first homes established for the destitute, infirm and old, as a direct result of legislation. They were financed by a poor rate which was determined and ordered by the justices. Under the Act of 1598, the overseer was directed to set to work, or apprentice, children of families unable to support them. He was empowered to set the able to work and to buy the necessary material – flax, hemp, wool, thread, iron, etc. Their produce was targeted to contribute to aiding the poor and, of course at the same time, hopefully to reduce the burden of the poor rate on the wealthier parishioners. If surplus profits were created they were to be used towards the relief of victims of fire, flood etc.

These Elizabethan poorhouses were the immediate forerunners of the workhouse. Usually small, they provided for both infirm aged people and many who were fit but found it hard to obtain work in the open market because they were likely to be a less profitable source of labour than younger men and women.

In 1623 an Act was passed to encourage the erection of hospitals and workhouses for the poor. Reading, Sheffield and Cambridge were among the first towns to establish large workhouses to play a part in the growing textile industry. The one in Cambridge was known as the Spinning House, but most were little more than workshops.

Towards the end of the sixteenth century and in the early seventeenth century, many other attempts were made to provide for the destitute and aged by finding employment for the able-bodied through the creation of various work schemes. 'Corporations of the Poor' were formed: their object was to relieve destitution and starvation through the industry of the poor themselves instead of depending upon a more equable distribution of wealth through taxing better-off parishioners by means of the poor rate. These community work schemes aimed at putting materials into the hands of the destitute and organising them to produce saleable goods. Paupers were provided with food and shelter and those able to work were sometimes hired out to local employers. Proceeds from these activities were used to finance the inmates' shelter and sustenance.

Apart from relieving the local authorities of the cost of their sustenance, paupers were regarded by some as providing an attractive source of labour. In 1660, Thomas Lawson proposed to parliament that each parish should make special efforts to supply paupers to work for local manufacturers and appoint someone to do this. His recommendation included the establishment of an Employment Exchange. Most of the schemes, however, were aimed purely at benefiting the paupers. In 1669 George Fox advised fellow Quakers to set up a house or houses so that a hundred paupers could have rooms to work in, shops where their products could be sold, and where widows and young women could work and live.

In 1696, another remarkable Quaker, John Bellers, whose writing and work influenced Lawson, Fox, Karl Marx, Francis Place and Robert Owen, published his *Proposals for Raising a College of Industry*. His 'college' was an independent cooperative in which poor people could live and work. Bellers thought that they should largely administer themselves and be free from the constant competition of the capitalist economy. He suggested that it was in the interest of the rich to educate and take care of the poor. He pointed out that the rich depended upon the poor 'if one had a hundred acres of land ... and as many cattle, without a labourer, what would the rich man be, but a labourer?'

Although his plan for a residential college of industry was not realised, Bellers became the financial adviser to another successful Quaker work scheme in 1680. This was started in 1677, initially by raising £100 which was used to buy flax for Quaker poor to spin at home or in prison.[7]

[7]T.V. Hitchcock (ed.) Richard Hutton's Complaint Book, The Notebook of the Steward of the Quaker Workhouse at Clerkenwell, 1711–1737, London Record Society, 1987.

In 1690, John Cary, Robert Clayton, Rowland Vaughan, and Thomas Firmin established the 'Samuel Hartlib Foundation of the Corporation of the Poor of London'. Between 1696 and 1711, 14 more corporations were formed. The most notable was the one in Bristol where stone breaking was the main occupation of men. The work allocated to women was knitting and lace making. It was founded by an Act of Parliament in 1696 through the efforts of John Cary. This Act permitted 19 parishes to cooperate in order to establish a workhouse instead of having to limit their activity to their own parish.

Even though a great deal of support for the formation of these corporations was in the belief that being larger enterprises they would be more economical to run and consequently reduce the poor rate burden, the first workhouses were opened as havens for the poor where shelter, food and dignity could be secured through labour. This enlightened, if austere, concept of the workhouse did not last long.

The rates raised by churchwardens to help the poor and aged survive were based upon property values and rents. In view of the current fervent debate on the council tax, we shouldn't be surprised that these taxes, not always fairly assessed, were resented. For example, in 1711 the parish of Farmington, London, collected about three pence a week from house residents in Fleet Street, but Sir Richard Hoar who owned two houses in Mitre Court in the same parish was charged two shillings per week. Opposition to the actual amount of the rates and ways of reducing them were a common subject for public discussion.

A pamphlet against 'the unfair poor rate' was published by Peter Boursot in 1739.[8] He was rated at threepence a week (three shillings and threepence per quarter) by the Parish of St Botolph's, Aldergate. He argued that his whole estate amounted to no more than £50 and that his rate was not fair in proportion to that raised from others. He cited the case of a Mr Quilter worth £7,000 to £8,000 who was rated at seven shillings a quarter and a Mr Wood worth £5,000 to £6,000 rated at five shillings a quarter. In spite of his protests, on 12 April 1737 the churchwarden seized goods including 'dice and draughtboards' from Peter Boursot in lieu of arrears of eight shillings.

---

[8] P. Boursot, *Poor Honesty's Fight with Two Parishes*, Guildhall Library, 1739.

Those like Mr Boursot, anxious to save their money, naturally supported the work schemes being put forward by reformers such as John Cary, Robert Clayton, Rowland Vaughan and Thomas Firmin. Firmin spoke out against sending paupers to the factories. He wanted materials and support to be given to the poor who could work in their own homes, leaving residential shelter to homeless beggars and vagrants.

Matthew Marryott, a country gentleman, was an ardent advocate of the deterrent aspect of the workhouse. He made a small fortune from managing parish workhouses, and several larger establishments in the south east like the Westminster workhouse which accommodated 302 inmates. Marryott strongly supported the Workhouse Test Act, of 1723 sponsored by Sir Edward Knatchbull. Its full title was 'For Amending the Laws relating to the Settlement, Employment and Relief of the Poor' (9 Geo. I c. vii). It authorised any parish to set up its own workhouse, stressing that ideally it should form a deterrent to seeking poor relief, forcing the poor to seek any avenue for existence before resorting to the parish. Parish authorities lost no time in cooperating with Knatchbull. Between 1723 and 1732, 300 workhouses were set up. By 1750 more than 600 were in existence. The elderly along with the adults were mostly employed in oakum picking, (untwisting fibres of old rope used to caulk ship timber joints); the children, who also received a very primary education, were engaged in spinning. Most parishes claimed that the result was large savings in the poor rates. The Act of 1723 also ruled that management of workhouses, previously operated by the parishes, could be contracted out to private persons. The successful bidder would be entitled to any profit that could be made out of fee paid by the parish. Naturally, running costs were minimised, generally resulting in harsh regimes.

For instance, the Nacton 'House of Industry' was opened in 1756. It was estimated that in its first four years, £2,000 was cut from the local costs incurred in sustaining paupers. Parish poor rates were halved. The workhouse was becoming a movement to contain the costs incurred by paupers claiming indoor relief rather than the means of providing a dignified, if basic, home for the destitute. In fact, entering Nacton workhouse was dreaded by the poor of Suffolk and, in 1765, faced with having to choose between the Nacton workhouse or go without relief, they demonstrated so energetically that they had to be quelled by a force of dragoons.[9]

Nevertheless, life for the poor and destitute on the outside was grim and many tried to gain admission to the workhouse in order to be assured of essential shelter and food. The authorities quickly concluded that the numbers admitted would only be limited to manageable and affordable proportions if life *inside* the workhouse was made harsh and punitive enough to discourage applicants. Furthermore, it was reckoned that the introduction of a more intensive work regime would increase the 'profits' produced through the labours of the inmates, thus assisting the parish, or unions of parishes, in reducing the mounting costs of sustaining the poor.

Moves were made to make workhouses more uninviting. This was to have a dramatic effect on the aged poor. In the late eighteenth century, the expense of providing the workhouse inmate with even the most basic food and shelter was more than that incurred by the provision of 'outside' relief. The number of workhouse inmates was increasing and by 1777 had reached more than 1 per cent of the total population (the equivalent of 600,000 today). The pressure to make the workhouse a cruel and hard last resort was increased. It is difficult to appreciate the scale of the suffering endured by the poor, especially the aged poor, which forced them to resort to shelter inside its cold walls.

In 1753, the year before he died, Henry Fielding, the author of *Tom Jones*, published a proposal for making effectual provision for the poor and 'for amending their morals' through work.[10] He contended that 'the strength and riches of a society consisted through the numbers of its people, and that all depended upon the universal contribution of labour because nine-tenths of products are the result of labour'. Fielding concluded that government had an obligation to procure the means of labour and then to compel the idle to undertake it because 'Nature demands every individual to provide for the incapacities of infancy, illness and old age.' Henry Fielding was one of a growing number of intellectuals who believed in solving poverty through work schemes. He was of the opinion that a too-comfortable residential relief might dissuade some

---

[9]. N. Longmate, *The Workhouse*, Temple Smith, London, 1974.

[10] H. Fielding, A Proposal for making effectual Provision for the Poor, for amending their Morals and for rendering them useful Members of the Society, London, 1753.

hardened paupers from seeking work. He was behind a plan for building a huge workhouse for 5,000 paupers in Middlesex which was to rent out pauper labour to employers within a radius of 20 miles.

Faced with the problem of growing numbers of vagrants and paupers, the government favoured these work schemes and supported their extension. By the time of the Gilbert Act in 1782, two or more parishes were allowed to combine resources to establish workhouses. At this time the number of destitute had increased greatly and in an effort to reduce the numbers of those actually living in and the costs they incurred, every inmate was forced to labour. Only the old, sick and infirm, were excused. Other paupers were set to work in the parish, their earnings going towards their maintenance. If earnings were in excess of that required for their maintenance, then the surplus was to be given to them when accounts were made up each month. Setting paupers to work was still the main objective. If the able-bodied refused to work, they could be sent to a house of correction for a period of between one and three months.

About this time, the poor were taking matters into their own hands in France. In England the knowledge of what was happening just over the Channel, combined with the riots and the rick-burning taking place here, gave grave concern to landowners and undoubtedly prompted new initiatives aimed to placate the poor.

On 6 May 1795 an interesting initiative for relieving poverty was established by local squires in the Pelican Inn, Speenhamland, Newbury, in Berkshire. The 'Speenhamland Plan' was rooted in the belief that everyone had a right to a 'comfortable support'. (At its heart, it had much in common with the Beveridge report which was to appear 147 years later.) At the time, bread represented about two-thirds of the daily diet of the labouring class. The level of the 'poor relief' in the plan was calculated according to the cost of wheat and bread. It ruled that every man should have two one-gallon loaves,[11] each weighing 8 lbs 11 ounces, every week plus a shilling. In addition, each should receive a one-gallon loaf[12] plus six pence for his wife and each child. The cost amounted to

---

[11] M. Neuman, The Speenhamland County, Poverty and the Poor Laws in Berkshire 1782–1834, Garland Publishing, New York and London, 1982.

[12] One gallon of flour, 6 oz butter, pint of yeast, a little salt, two yolks and one white of egg, in Elizabeth Raffald, *The Experienced English Housekeeper*, London, 1808.

three shillings per week for a single person plus one shilling and sixpence for each dependant. Moreover, it was stated that this should be the minimum standard for every man whether unemployed or at work.

In this way, an income to provide a basic living was to be provided to all. It was a very early, and albeit local, move to establish a basic minimum wage, the level of which was to be indexed to the price of bread. If a worker's earnings fell below the Speenhamland standard then parish relief could be claimed to make up the difference. As a result, a farmer paying very low wages would be under peer pressure to raise them as otherwise the difference between them and the Speenhamland rate affected the level of the poor rate. The Speenhamland scale was frequently referred to as a basis for establishing rates of relief throughout the country. As well as a harbinger of the minimum wage, Speenhamland had also ruled that poor relief as well as the local minimum wage was to be linked to prices. However, the Speenhamland benefit rate did not fundamentally alter the desperately sad life of thousands of poor people nationwide, including the sick or aged who, through no fault of their own, were unable to work.

At the turn of the century, many other schemes for sustaining the growing numbers of the poor were advanced. In 1819, Thomas Wright proposed to create a 'Small Farm Society' with capital provided by £10 shares. His idea was to establish a number of smallholdings of between four and twelve acres each with a cottage.[13] He calculated that six of these in every parish nationwide would provide enough bread for a total of 343,000 souls. Thomas Wright's plan aimed to abolish *poverty* whereas most of the plans put into effect by the government were aimed at abolishing *paupers*. This remained the object of a great number of less philanthropic people who believed that laziness and lack of initiative were the cause of poverty, and that society should be wary of 'interfering' with the condition of the destitute by action prompted by compassion and charity.

One example of this attitude can be found in a pamphlet published in 1816 (*A View of the Cause of our Late Prosperity and of our Present Distress and of the Means which have been proposed for our Relief*). This held that: 'The

[13] Thomas Wright, Plan for the Salvation of the Country, the Prevention of Crime, to give Bread and Employment to the Poor and a Greater Supply of Provisions to the Weekly Markets, 1819, The Philanthropic Society, St George's Fields, London.

effect of statutes for relief of the poor, upon the community, appears to diminish the necessity for economising the expenditure of food among the lower classes of society ... and by removing the necessity for exertion and frugality to render them indolent and wasteful ...' . James Ebenezer Bicheno was firmly of this point of view. He opposed any generous provision for the poor. In 1817, he wrote an article which appeared in the journal *Inquiry* maintaining that 'Every brute beast reproduces without regard to food available and that this was a perfectly acceptable law of nature for, although the resultant competition for resources between these beasts did result in death for some, it was inevitable and welcome because if there were always enough food, instincts and abilities which lead to improvement would wither. The lion would no longer possess his strength, the horse its swiftness, the fox its cunning.' This was a forthright 'survival of the fittest' argument and advocacy of the virtues of competition, hardly likely to favour the aged poor. The non-ambiguity of Mr Bicheno's view might well find sympathy amongst today's proponents of the free market and the individual's prime role of self-interest.

Mr Bicheno was by no means alone in his beliefs. It was common in Victorian times for the 'respectable' to profess that the poor themselves were basically responsible for, and should be blamed for, their condition, and that the giving of alms encouraged idleness. Many seemed ready to accept a return to values of the 1500s when giving to able-bodied beggars was illegal. In his *History of the Poor Law*, Dr Barn stated that 'If none were to give, none would beg and the whole mystery and craft would be at an end in a fortnight'. Presumably, he believed poverty too would equally be abolished by this simple discipline.

The establishment was naturally influenced by all of this and took great pains to lay emphasis on the importance of ensuring that recipients of any relief were 'deserving' and 'of good character'.

From the street to the workhouse

God bless the squire and his relations
And keep me in my proper station
God made bees, the bees make honey
The paupers do the work
And the Guardians get the money
I am compelled to sit and hear
What the parson says while standing here
He tells us we're miserable sinners
He'd be the same on workhouse dinners
But he is fat, like well-fed pork
He eats and drinks but does no work
We hear him promise that when we die
There'll be great helpings
Of pie in the sky
Then he shuts his book
And slings his hook

                                    Amen

(Poem found scratched on inside of a workhouse desk)

The early 1800s were a time of unrest. The 'Roberts Mule' spinner introduced in 1825 could spin cotton fibres 370 times faster than a hand spinner, and its introduction profoundly affected the life of thousands of workers. Although employment in the textile mills was increasing, large-scale domestic production, in which older members of the family participated, was hit heavily. Earnings were forced down to a bare subsistence level. The years between 1811 and 1816 saw Luddites sabotaging the machinery that was displacing textile workers in the Midlands and the North. In 1830, the Captain Swing riots[14] led to the destruction of 387 threshing machines that had brought unemployment to many agricultural workers and the protest burning of barns. A popular 'Swing' poem at the time declared: 'They could not see our miseries: light them thus, Mayhap they'll read them by yon granary's flame'.[15] Rural workers began to join together in protesting at the starvation wages they were being paid. In 1834, six farm labourers from Tolpuddle were sentenced to seven years' transportation for administering illegal oaths while founding a trade union in Dorset.[16] In the same year the Chartist movement was formed. Troops were in common use to control riots and demonstrations.

Between 1801 and 1843 the total population of England and Wales had almost doubled from 8,872,980 to 15,906,829. Nearly 10 per cent (1,539,490) were destitute, and a large proportion of these poor people were elderly. A result of industrialisation was that many were concentrated in the towns without the local and family ties of the village poor. Traditional help and support from the parish were not available. As a consequence, life was difficult, and frequently the struggle was simply to stay alive. If unable to obtain assistance or steal, the poor would be without shelter and end up starving and dying on the street.

As discussed above, one alternative was the workhouse. While some were genuine attempts to shelter the most unfortunate in the community, the majority of institutions were in fact established to reduce local poor rates. A study carried out in the late 1700s by Sir Frederick Eden's (*The State of the Poor*) had shown that in 1797 only a few Poor Law institutions were clean and well run. The majority were overcrowded and cruelly administered. Nepotism in appointment of officers, corruption and malpractices were rife. The worst institutions were mostly small and in rural areas. In these, the well, sick, young, aged and 'lunatics' were all invariably confined in close proximity. The workhouse was not providing the poor with a decent and civilised place to shelter.

---

[14] E. Hobsbawn and G. Rude, *Captain Swing*, Lawrence & Wishart, 1969.

[15] 'Swing' a poem, *The English Republic*, 1851, p.276.

[16] J. Marlow, *The Tolpuddle Martyrs*, Andre Deutsch, 1971.

The Whig government's Poor Law Act of 1834 was an effort to improve the efficiency of poor relief and to regularise it throughout the country. Termed the 'Amendment and Better Administration of Laws relating to the Poor in England and Wales', the Act ensured greater control over the appointment of officers and their accountability. In addition, on the premise that anyone accepting relief in a workhouse must lack the will to support themselves, workhouse rules and regimes were tightened. Outside poor relief, which had been administered by justices and churchwardens (some of whom who were considered to be too generous to the able-bodied poor) was now taken over by Boards of Guardians who were drawn from the aristocracy, local landowners, gentry and magistrates.

This new Act had at its root the perception that *idleness*, not poverty, was the problem. And idleness had to be eradicated. The Act's objective was to force idle and people of 'low moral fibre' to work. It held that destitution was the responsibility, not of the community, but of the destitute themselves and that their redemption lay through austerity and hard labour. This coloured the treatment of old and young poor alike. Workhouse regime, accommodation and diets are recorded in great detail in various parliamentary papers of 1844. Cold rules and factual accounts convey the tragic circumstances in which so many older people lived out their final years. The core principle of the workhouse was no longer philanthropic.

The regions responsible for the poor were extended from the parish to 'unions of parishes'. Each union contained more than 50,000 inhabitants. Hundreds of new workhouses were built during the nineteenth century. In spite of the legislation of 1834 to encourage parishes to unite their resources to build larger and well-laid out workhouses and to reform their administration, life inside was cruel and the administration was often corrupt. The workhouse now played a deterrent role rather than acting as a haven for the needy. For those few who were destitute because of idleness or drink, this may have been valid, but for the unfortunate who had to resort to the workhouse due to old age it is difficult to appreciate how the deterrent was supposed to be effective. Corruption and maladministration were rife and the life of an inmate was harsh and provided nothing beyond mere survival.

The House of Commons 1837 Committee to 'Enquire into the Operation and Effect of the Poor Law Amendment Act' heard evidence from a 47-year-old labourer, Henry Sopp, who told the committee that two of his seven children were in the workhouse. He and his wife had to manage on nine shillings and sixpence per week.[17] Edwin Chapman, however testified that – in his view – a man could live on six shillings per week.

We get some idea of the cruelty of the new Poor Law in the fact that it legislated that no applicant should be admitted into the workhouse if suffering from serious maladies. A parish medical officer Mr David Wilson recounted[18] what had happened when he was called upon to examine a naked woman afflicted with a malignant fever. As a consequence of the fever, she and her child had been turned out of the hovel in which they were sheltering. When the woman applied to Chelsea for relief, the relieving officer gave her a ticket for bread after abusing her; but in her present weak state, Mr Wilson recorded that she could not eat bread and that:

> … the unfortunate creature is literally dying from starvation, and if immediate relief be not afforded her, I will not answer for the consequences. Her condition is of the most horrible character. She has not the slightest support – not the common necessaries of life. Medicine will not be of the slightest benefit to her without proper rest, quiet and nourishment, she should be sent to some asylum. In the course of my medical practice, I do not think I ever saw such an extreme case of exhaustion – in fact as I stated before, starvation.

The chairman however expressed his inability to order her admittance to the workhouse. There was evidence here of the moral code underlying practices dealing with the poor. The notion that those who would obtain assistance should be 'deserving' persisted. For instance, Herbert Smith, in a twopenny pamphlet published in 1838[19] declared: 'It is well to be borne in mind that the greatest cause of Poverty is immorality; and therefore,

---

[17] William Denison, Evidence taken before House of Commons committee February 27th 1837; G.B. Whittaker & Co. London.

[18] Henry Kent Causton, Historical Review of the Poor and Vagrant Laws from the earliest period on record to the present time affording data for legislation from experience, London, Birchin Lane, 1838.

[19] Herbert Smith B.A., An Account of the situation and treatment of the women with illegitimate children in the New Forest Union Workhouse with some suitable remarks on the sin of fornication and its consequences, London, Printed by W. Tyler, Bolt Court, Fleet Street, 1838.

the surest method of ameliorating the condition of the Poor, is by working at an improvement in their moral conduct.'

Nevertheless, there was considerable and influential opposition to the new Poor Law: tales of alleged cruelty in workhouses were published in *The Times* and *Blackwood's Magazine*. In 1844, it was recorded that starving paupers at the Andover Union Workhouse, engaged in bone crushing, were resorting to eat the marrow and remaining putrid flesh. An enquiry was held and its findings, which were published in *The Times*, stated that it disgraced the statute book. Following a number of cases of scandalous cruelty and mismanagement of workhouses, especially that of Andover, the Poor Law Commission was replaced by the Poor Law Authority which was directly responsible to parliament. The Authority made some improvements to institutional relief.

In 1847 when mobility of people to seek work outside their parish was becoming absolutely essential to provide labour for the growing number of factories, an amendment was made to the Poor Law that relaxed the restrictions on the movement of workers. It stated that 'the law of settlement and removal produces hardship by impeding circulation of labour ... and ... is injurious to employers and impedes agriculture'. This may have made it easier for unemployed people to seek work but it did not solve the unemployment problem. What it did do was increase migration to the industrial towns and exacerbate the difficulties of dealing with the destitute there.

We find a graphic account of the lot of the urban poor at that time in Charles Cochrane's *Poor Man's Guardian* (dated October 1847). This tells of a night visit made by Mr Jones, the Philanthropic Society's secretary, to St Martin's Workhouse in London. Mr Jones had been saddened to have seen inmates covered by rugs huddling together for warmth. They were completely naked because that made them less likely to catch the 'itch' or other diseases. These were the lucky ones. Nineteen people including children were observed to be spending that night on the cold pavement outside because the workhouse was full. Mr Jones commented, 'I left scarcely believing that in this wealthy and charitable metropolis, human beings were compelled to sleep in open streets from a want of that accommodation which even dogs and pigs have carefully provided for them'.[20]

---

[20] *The Poor Man's Guardian*, Saturday, 6 November 1847.

In 1859 a retired relieving officer wrote a book about the harshness of the Poor Laws and the inhumane manner in which they were administered.[21] Relating the story of Mary Farley, he told how she had given birth to her baby in Maidstone Gaol. After being released she made her way with her child to Gravesend and from there, by boat, to London ending up in Clerkenwell where she spent the night in a common lodging house. She desperately needed relief but, instead of claiming it from Clerkenwell, she walked on, carrying her baby, to claim it from another unnamed parish where she had previously resided. She made the journey because she thought that there she would be entitled to assistance without enduring the red tape and questioning to which she expected she would have been subjected to at Clerkenwell. She was, however, mistaken. The parish officials where she made the claim told her to go back to Clerkenwell and make a formal claim there. Then, they said, Clerkenwell could pass her back to them officially, probably in custody, and this would enable them to look into her case. Tired out and at the end of her tether Mary Farley went down to the river, threw her baby in and followed her. The baby was drowned. Mary Farley was pulled out of the water, arrested and charged with infanticide. She was convicted and transported for life to Australia.[22]

It's difficult to envisage the wretched conditions that poor older people endured in those times. Our visual impression of Victorian life comes from old films made in the last decade of the nineteenth century. They mainly recorded royal processions and funerals, people bustling around in town centres or promenading on the seafront. But in the 1830s, parish visitors to the Holborn workhouse reported finding 40 females aged from 40 to 80 in a small basement room built over a smelling sewer where, in semi-darkness, they worked 11 hours a day pulling wool for use in mattresses. Another account described old men and women, some of whom were bedridden, huddling together at night for warmth in draughty unheated and crowded quarters where they were kept awake by incessant coughing 'and other noises'. The regulations on uniforms, the lack of furniture, the absence of any privacy and, above all, the denial of companionship of a husband or wife in declining years combined to make for a desolate existence.

---

[21] Thomas Day, The Poor Laws Unmasked by a Late Relieving Officer, London, 1859.

[22] J.L. (J Lhtoky) late of the Colonial Service, On Cases of Death by Starvation, John Oliver, London 1844.

The gulf between rich and poor was growing fast. Philanthropic concern was combined with fear of disorder. Government action was called for. During the five years between 1834 and 1839, 350 workhouses were quickly built and many more between 1850 and 1860. This helped the destitute to obtain shelter and sustenance, removed numbers of paupers from the streets and attempted to counter the rapid increase of lawlessness.

It was impossible for most workers, even those who had regular employment, to save owing to low wages, and so most elderly people had nothing put by for their old age. During industrialisation family stability suffered and many old people were living alone without support. This made their condition pitiable. Many were hard put to assure themselves of other than a pauper's burial. Their last resort was the workhouse. Officially they became paupers. The word 'pauper' carried with it a sense of disgrace. It was used to describe destitute men and women of all ages, children and babies – even their graves. It denied human dignity. The term remained officially in use until 1948.

Throughout the nineteenth century the old among the inmates of the workhouse were present in proportions much greater than that of their age group in the population as a whole. The 1851 Census for Eastern Sussex showed that the workhouses at Battle, Brighton, Eastbourne, Lewes and Rye housed a total of 1,132 inmates of whom 263 were 60 years or older. There were 403 inmates under 15 years.[23] Therefore, the elderly paupers represented 23 per cent of the total inmates and 36 per cent of those over 15 years. The disproportionality of this is evident when these percentages are compared with the numbers of older people in England and Wales at that time. People of 60 years and over accounted for only 7.3 per cent of the total population, and 11.3 per cent of those 15 and over.[24]

The granting of poor relief under the current Poor Laws fell into two categories. 'Indoor relief' was given to those who passed the workhouse qualifying test. 'Outdoor relief' was given, *subject to good behaviour*, not only in cases of actual destitution but with the view of assisting the old

---

[23] M.J. Burchell, *Eastern Sussex Workhouse Census 1851*, Sussex Family History Group, London, Guildhall Library, Pam 14593, May 1978.

[24] B.R. Mitchell, *British Historical Statistics*, Cambridge University Press, 1988.

who were in a state of poverty. Good behaviour was an essential condition as was good character plus contributions from relatives legally liable and fair contribution from relatives not legally liable. The Board of Guardians could refuse outdoor relief when these conditions were unfulfilled. In 1892 whereas only 7.4 per cent of the population of England and Wales was over 60, almost 25 per cent were paupers receiving indoor, outdoor or medical relief.

Charles Booth (1840–1916) played a vital role in the campaign for the old age pensions. A successful businessman, he had been an ardent radical in his youth (even canvassing for the Liberal Party) but had subsequently become disillusioned with all political parties. Troubled by the harsh poverty of the times, he was to undertake profound and scientific surveys of the poor which underlined the desperate need for reform.[25] London's Stepney had more than its share of poverty and in 1887 Charles Booth made a comprehensive study of its workhouse population.[26] He examined inmates to discover reasons for their pauperism. Among the 23 classifications advanced by Booth as causes of inmates' resort to the workhouse were: 'Crime', 'Vice', 'Drink', 'Laziness', 'Pauper association', Heredity, Mental disease, Temper (queer), Incapacity, Early marriage (girl), Large family, Extravagance, Lack of work (unemployed), Trade misfortune, Restlessness (roving, tramp), No relations, Death of husband, Desertion (abandoned, widowed), Death of father or mother (orphan), Sickness, Accident, Ill luck as well as Old Age (60 plus). He concluded that the principal reason for pauperism was 'old age'. According to his survey this accounted for 33 per cent of those on indoor relief. Booth had listed 'old age' separately as a cause of being an inmate, whereas a detailed study of Booth's findings, reveals that 'old people' were to be found under other headings, so, for example, 57 per cent of those said to be admitted for drunkenness were 60 and over; and 41 per cent of those taken in because of sickness were also old, as were 58 per cent of the deserted or widowed and 75 per cent of those admitted because of 'unemployment' or, more interestingly, 'through having suffered trade misfortune'.

---

[25] The Aged Poor in England and Wales, Macmillan, 1894; Life and Labour of the People of London, Macmillan, 1903, etc.

[26] C. Booth, Pauperism, a Picture and the Endowment of Old Age, Macmillan, 1892.

Out of the 700 inmates, no less than 435 were aged 60 or older. This means that in fact 62.1 per cent of all inmates were 'old', much more than the 33 per cent listed by Booth. Moreover, of the adult inmates of 16 years and over, the percentage of old paupers was 67.8 per cent. From Charles Booth's findings it can be safely assumed that more than two-thirds of the Stepney adult workhouse inmates were over the age of 60. The real reason for them being there was undoubtedly due to their age even though the records had sometimes indicated other causes.

In the face of this evidence, even the meanest Victorian Scrooge couldn't justify the proposition that those in the workhouse were mainly lazy layabouts, and that they were there largely through their own fault. It pointed to the fact that only those in the extremes of destitution reluctantly sought admittance and that the old were a high proportion of those poor souls.

Alcohol was considered to be one of the main threats to the happiness of the working classes and Victorian reformers and philanthropists were greatly preoccupied with the fight against the vice of drunkenness. Drinking was seen as a sin responsible for, rather than an escape from, a life of poverty. Temperance societies flourished. One of these was the Band of Hope, which was dedicated to influencing children against the evils of drink. Two other key concerns of reformers were lack of thrift and laziness although these three categories together allegedly accounted for less than 20 per cent of all the paupers in Stepney. The fact that, compared to Outdoor Relief, Indoor Relief was expensive led to a strong measures to reduce the numbers qualifying for it. The strictest supervision of its administration was demanded. The workhouse was designed to be a deterrent to the indolent rather than a haven for the unfortunate

Modelled upon the prison system, a uniform dress was adopted. The inmates, including the elderly who, had to obey many rules. Sexes were segregated, husbands separated from wives. Movement within the walls was controlled and permission was required to make visits to the world outside. In many workhouses old people were not even allowed to brew themselves a cup of tea. Rules were laid down by government which aimed to prevent the worst excesses of the institutions' administration.[27]

[27] Order of the Poor Law Commissioners to the Unions of Ireland, *Workhouse Rules*, Parliamentary Papers 1844, **40**.

These covered: 'admissions', 'classification of inmates', 'discipline', 'paupers' diets', and 'visits'. They also defined the duties of master, matron, schoolmaster and schoolmistress, porter, medical officer and chaplain.

Once paupers had passed the 'test' of the need and right to enter the workhouse, they were allowed admission if they presented himself within three days of a written order from the guardians or, in urgent cases, at the discretion and on the authority of, the workhouse master or matron. As soon as admitted, a pauper's name and religion were recorded and he or she was placed in a probationary ward and had to wait there for an examination by the medical officer. Before removal from the probationary ward it was ruled that 'the pauper shall be thoroughly cleansed and clothed in a workhouse dress'. Original clothes were labelled after purification to be restored on discharge.

Paupers were classified under five headings: (1) males above 15 years; (2) boys between 2 and 15 years; (3) females over 15; (4) girls 2 to 15; and (5) children under 2 years. They were separated, 'Each class, ... shall respectively remain in the apartment assigned to them, without communication with any other class'. The exceptions to this rule were aged persons and females and girls acting as nurses or household helps (but household helps were not permitted to communicate with boys and males). Girls and boys under 15 were allowed to meet in school. The benevolence of the system was illustrated by the rules that permitted mothers to be with their children under 2 years of age and to have access to their children aged between 2 and 7 years at all reasonable times. Moreover, the master of the workhouse, subject to the local guardians' regulations, was to allow any father or mother 'to have an interview with a child at some time each day'.

Discipline was rigid. The elderly were not allowed tobacco or liquor. If silence was ordered, to break it was considered a punishable offence as was use of bad language, uncleanliness, playing cards, pretending sickness, neglect or refusal to work or entering or attempting to enter an area designated for a different class of pauper. Punishment for breaking the rules varied from increased working hours to reduced diets and solitary confinement. It was also necessary to control the staff's enthusiasm to punish offenders. It was ruled that no child was to be confined in a dark room overnight, and corporal punishment, on boys only, was to be solely administrated by means of a rod or other instrument approved by the Board of Guardians.[28] For those over 15 years of age, the punishment for a first offence was an extra hour of work for two days; for a repeated offence the penalty was confinement for up to 24 hours, with or without extra work or restricted diet. However, if the offender was over 60 years of age diet was not to be restricted.

In the summer of 1851, over 250,000 starving people in Ireland found shelter and food in the workhouse. A typical day's diet in the Antrim workhouse was a breakfast of 6 ounces of oatmeal 'made into a stirabout' plus one-third of a quart of buttermilk; dinner was 7 ounces of Indian meal stirabout plus one- third of a quart of buttermilk; supper was 4 ounces of Indian meal stirabout (porridge) plus one-third of a quart of buttermilk. Occasionally, brown bread and meat and vegetable soup was provided as an alternative dinner.[29]

Whilst better than starvation – indeed, the diets were set to include between 160 and 170 ounces of solid food per week which was one-third more than that of the average agricultural worker – life in British workhouses was just a miserable survival. However, it actually conferred a degree of respectability above that associated with those on outside poor relief.

Nevertheless, even this right to survival was not always available due to the lack of accommodation and an overriding desire to limit costs. For instance, although he had been born in the parish and was entitled to relief, William Williams, 76 years old, and suffering from a hernia was turned out of Whitechapel's parish workhouse in 1856. He had no relatives and had maintained himself by manual labouring up to his admission three months earlier. Whilst in the workhouse he had worked occasionally picking oakum for five hours a day. Then, after only three months of indoor relief, he was discharged on to the street to fend for himself. Fortunately for him, Mr Martin, a member of the Corn Exchange, took up his case and attended the magistrate's court with him to help present his petition for readmission. He was eventually readmitted. In the course of the hearing it was disclosed that a notice had been posted

---

[28] Four Orders of the Poor Law Commissioners to Unions in Ireland, Parliamentary Papers 1844, **40**.

[29] *Gaols and Workhouses (Ireland)*, Parliamentary Papers, 13 July, 1848.

over the gates of the workhouse to the effect that from 23 August 1856 the casual ward would be closed and no person would be admitted. It was suggested that this might explain why three persons had recently been found dead or dying in the streets nearby from exhaustion and exposure.

Many wealthy and influential people were becoming increasingly disturbed by the inhumane treatment of the poor. In the preface to Charles Dickens' first edition of *Martin Chuzzlewit* in 1844, he wrote 'Let the reader go into the children's side of any prison in England, or, I grieve to add, of many workhouses, and judge whether those are monsters who disgrace our streets, people our hulks and penitentiaries, and overcrowd our penal colonies, or are creatures whom we have deliberately suffered to be bred for misery and ruin.'

The Gilbert Act of 1792 had permitted outside relief to be given to the able-bodied poor, and had been intended to retain the workhouse itself as a home for the sick and old. That was rarely the case. The aged inmates were usually mixed with others and, whilst not expected to work, they experienced the same regime as the other destitute. Moreover, whereas the able-bodied younger paupers might harbour the belief that one day they would have an opportunity to leave, the elderly realised that they would invariably end their lives there. By 1815 there were nearly one million paupers in Britain, of whom some 10 per cent were workhouse inmates.

After 1850 the view that older paupers were a special case in themselves gained support. It was seen to be unjust that destitute old persons of blameless character who had worked all their lives should lose their civil rights and suffer the stigma of pauperism. One way to avoid officially classifying them as paupers would be for the state to award them a pension, instead of poor relief. This, it was argued, would not only redress an injustice but reduce the amount spent on indoor relief.

In 1891, the population was 29,001,018. The records show that in the year1890/9, just over 4.5 per cent of the population were paupers (1,317,104), and that 31 per cent of them were over 60 years of age. However, what is noteworthy is that people over 60 accounted for only 7.4 per cent of the total population. From this, it is clear that a person reaching 60 (no mean achievement in those hard times), ran a much higher risk of becoming destitute than a younger adult. The odds against living to 60 were 14 to 1 against. Those who beat those odds were likely to end up in the workhouse – if there was room! The workhouse[30] had become the state's method of 'caring' for the elderly.

---

[30] A post-1834 catalogue of more than 700 workhouses, outside of metropolitan London, together with their locations is given in K. Morrison, *The Workhouse – A Study of Poor-Law Buildings in England*, English Heritage, 1999.

Pensions not poor relief

'It is not charity but a right – not bounty but justice,
that I am pleading for'   Thomas Paine

Before 1908, apart from a few officials and members of the armed forces, hardly anyone reaching the end of their working life had a pension on which to base their retirement. As we have seen, those who lived beyond their active years relied on charity to save them from starvation. Invariably, the aged depended upon their family and friends and, if these were poor or had come upon hard times, there was little available for them. The vast majority of older people suffered extreme hardship which could only be alleviated by charity, most of which, as we saw above, was provided by the church. From time to time, various plans were put forward to cater for the aged, but few were practical or implemented.

As far back as the thirteenth century, Roger Bacon had urged that a public fund should be maintained to support 'those who are not able to make a living owing to infirmity or old age'. He suggested this could be funded by 'fines extracted by the state and from the confiscated property of rebels'.[31] Another early scheme to care for impoverished gentlefolk (Lloyds 'names' may be interested to note), was initiated by Jean le Bou of France. In 1351, he established the 'Chivalric Order of the Star' to care for 'old knights' so that they could be treated with respect in their old age and each be provided with two servants to look after them.

In the late eighteenth century, as national wealth hugely increased as a result of emerging industrialisation and growing trade, more all-

---

[31] *Opers Majes, Roger Bacon*, English translation by R.B. Burke, Vol. II, Part 2, p.661, Philadelphia,1928.

embracing proposals surfaced for the sustenance of the old and destitute, beyond that provided by the church and charitable individuals. One of the earliest plans to provide state security for old people was that proposed in *Agrarian Justice* by Thomas Paine in 1796. He urged that a national fund should be established to finance a scheme of old pensions for all in need, enabling them 'to live in old age without wretchedness, and go decently out of the world'. He proposed that the annual pension should be £6 at age 50 and £10 at 60, and that the fund should be raised through a land inheritance tax. Regrettably, the plan was not seriously considered and sadly Tom Paine died in near poverty 13 years later at the age of 73. The sole dignity of his own departure lay in the fighting spirit that never deserted him.[32]

By the beginning of the nineteenth century the increasing number of destitute people in the expanding urban industrial areas had become a critical problem. Ten per cent of the population were without proper shelter and food. Revolutionary France was but a score of miles away; small wonder that civil unrest was perceived by the establishment as a threat.

The problem of the elderly poor was not given special consideration. Of course, they were not numerous. The expectation of life was low. Less than 50 per cent of men aged 20 years could expect to reach 60.[32] Those who did were expected to have accumulated sufficient savings and resources to live on. Actually, unless they were fortunate to have been born into a well-off family, or had been successful in trade, few were so blessed. The vast majority of older people had little to fall back on. As shown above, alone or from poor families with nothing to spare, they depended entirely upon charitable relief. While the church, philanthropists and humanitarian societies did much to relieve their suffering and to keep them from starving in the fields and streets, the elderly poor received the same help as everyone else. They were not a special case.

The Victorian conscience was stirred. Novelists Charles Dickens, Elizabeth Gaskell and Benjamin Disraeli wrote sympathetically about the urban poor. Charitable aid substantially increased at this time when

[32] P. Johnson, Saving and Spending, The Working Class Economy in Britain 1870–1939, Clarendon Press, 1985.

national resources, although fast growing, were much less than today. There was growing public awareness that a large proportion of old people on relief had worked hard all their lives and were poor through no fault of their own. It was becoming acknowledged that low wages had made it impossible for them to provide adequately for their latter years when frailty prevented them from earning their bread and hearth. To saddle these unfortunate aged people with the reproach associated with the label 'pauper' together with the loss of any civil rights they may have possessed, was seen to be unjust. Enlightened people thought that these elderly poor should be assisted by providing them with a pension and that this should be available to them by right of their having attained an age when frailty alone made them unable to provide for themselves. There was no state pension. So, in the early 1800's a movement developed to reduce , if not end, the dependence of the old and infirm upon their families or charity.

In 1842 Londoner Benjamin Steill published a broadsheet addressed to the '1500 Sensible Citizens of London who elect 206 Common Councilmen'. His objective was to gain support for his campaign to reduce the yearly £150,000 expenditure of the lord mayor and his officials, and to use the savings made to benefit elderly poor of the city through a pension scheme. Benjamin Steill proposed to reduce the pay of the Lord Mayor by £2,000 or £3,000, dismiss the allegedly inactive town clerk and discontinue printing session papers. He proposed to use the £6,000 he reckoned would thus be saved annually to provide 100 citizens with pensions of £30 per year, 100 at £20 and a further 100 widows with £10 per year.[33] He pointed out that the budgeted £150 for the Lord Mayor's Annual November 9th Dinner for ministers, judges, bishops, ambassadors and other dignitaries would 'if I were on a Union Workhouse stool instead of filling a Civic Chair, pay my board and lodging and for 6,300 dinners'. It would be interesting to learn how many dinners for the city's homeless the money spent on the Lord Mayor's Annual Banquet at the Mansion House would pay for today.

In 1878 the journal *Nineteenth Century* published an article by Canon William Blackley. This article outlined his ideas for a national insurance and pension plan. Canon Blackley was concerned with what he saw as

---

[33] *To the 1500 Sensible Citizens of London who elect 206 Common Council Men to spend for them £150,000 a year,* a broadsheet by Benjamin Steill, 20 Paternoster Row, Dec.1842, Guildhall Library, L41.191,B'side 1657.

'the pinch of old age being matched by lavish expenditure in youth preceding marriage'. He proposed a compulsory scheme for all workers between 18 and 21 years. They should, he believed, contribute from their annual wages a total of £10 to an annuity fund. He proposed that employers should be compelled by law to ensure contributions were made. This, with a top-up from the state, would provide sick insurance of eight shillings per week and a pension of four shillings weekly at 70. Canon Blackley argued that this pension scheme would reduce the poor rate substantially.[34]

Charles Booth credited Blackley with being the first person to propose a contributory national pension scheme for the elderly. At the time, of a total population of 34.5 million about one million (2.9 per cent) were over 70. Canon Blackley's suggested, that his plan was feasible providing that two-thirds of the 1,570,000 male youths in the United Kingdom at that time were employed at wages sufficient to enable them to contribute. The proposal gained some support but was never realised. It was opposed by the very influential friendly societies.[35] There were over 20,000 registered societies all over the country with grand names like Hearts of Oak and the Ancient Order of Foresters. Most of higher paid workers were members who, for less than eight pence per week, would be entitled to ten shillings weekly sick pay, a doctor's attendance and a funeral allowance. The friendly societies, concerned with their own financial position, regarded any form of state insurance as encroaching upon their territory and threatening their interests. They remained for many years powerful opponents of state pensions.

Blackley's scheme was pronounced technically unsound by a select committee of the Commons in 1887. However, it was regarded sympathetically by many philanthropists, including Charles Booth although he really wanted to see a national non-contributory old age pension scheme as the means of combating the widespread destitution of the elderly. Canon Blackley went on to become director of the Clergy Mutual Insurance Company, and was to become a leading light in organising insurance schemes for the clergy. Ironically, when legislation

---

[34] W.L. Blackley, 'National Insurance: A Cheap, Practical and Popular Means of Abolishing Poor Rates', *Nineteenth Century*, 4, November 1878.

[35] An early history of friendly societies is given in P.H. Gosden, *The Friendly Societies of England, 1815–1875*, Manchester Unity, 1961.

for non-contributory pensions was being drafted later, Canon Blackley opposed it. He had come to the view that the more urgent problem to be solved was the consumption of drink and tobacco by the poor.

In 1892, Charles Booth proposed that the state should provide a universal non-contributory pension of five shillings per week at age 65. This scheme for a non-contributory old age pension was not greeted enthusiastically by the establishment – the prevailing attitude was still that survival should depend upon hard work and thrift. Even Booth himself was influenced by these Victorian values in so far as he believed that 'drunkards, prostitutes and criminals ought to suffer, beyond the punishment such as the law provides, all the natural consequences of their conduct short of actually perishing from cold and hunger'. Clearly, as far as he was concerned, these fallen souls should be excluded from the full benefits of his proposed plan.

In spite of all the opposition, signs of progress towards old age pensions were becoming evident. An interesting non-contributory pension plan was initiated by the Borough of Deptford in 1893. This was funded by charitable donations, mainly from church collections and donations at annual festival dinners. The pension income was generated from those funds.[36] The scheme was to pension borough residents who reached the age of 60 years providing they had paid poor rates for at least seven years and had not received poor relief for four years prior to reaching 60. They had to be deserving. Men received twenty-six shillings and women twenty-two shillings monthly. Awarding of the pensions and the control of the scheme were in the hands of the subscribers. In 1893 there were nine Borough of Deptford pensioners; in 1903, they had increased to 42, when the total cost of providing pensions was £519 per year. By then, the invested fund had reached £2,700, the balance between income earned and the costs being made up by donations. In 1935, the fund was £23,079 and the number of pensioners had increased to 61.

Only a small number of old people were catered for by these early schemes. Generally, the beneficiaries had to be fortunate enough to have been in regular employment right up to retirement and, with rare exception, had never been in need of poor relief. These conditions meant that the vast majority of elderly people were excluded from being

---

[36] Borough of Deptford Pension Society, Guildhall Library, Pam 12151.

accepted into the few pension schemes in existence.

The presence of so many destitute older people in this rapidly growing wealthy nation was troubling increasing numbers of people. In a speech made on 7 December 1894, Joseph Chamberlain noted that 'of all men belonging to the working and poorer classes, one in two and a quarter (nearly one in two) is compelled under our present system, if he lives to 65, to have recourse to parish relief'. He had earlier commented that 'It must be remembered that it is almost impossible for a large proportion of the poorer classes to make adequate provision against old age.'[37] It was obvious that 'saving for old age' was not a practical solution for working people, and as Charles Booth had stated in his *Pauperism and the Endowment of Old Age*, 'women have often spent lives of the most active and invaluable citizenship, without ever having the smallest opportunity for saving.'

By the latter part of the nineteenth century, friendly societies were beginning, on a modest scale, to extend their cover from sick pay and funeral costs to superannuation. Germany passed a 'Law of Insurance against Old Age and Infirmity' in 1889. The Danes started a state pension system in 1891. New Zealand adopted non-contributory old age pensions in 1898. Rapidly industrialising Britain, with precious few private pension schemes, was clearly being left behind.

Several trade unions initiated superannuation schemes for their members, and by 1905 there were 39 trade union schemes covering 15,604 pensioners. All these schemes were contributory. Nonetheless, it was becoming clear that only a state scheme could properly address the national problem, and in the 1890s parliament began to examine the situation in earnest by means of specially appointed committees.

One such committee was a royal commission set up in 1893. Presided over by Lord Aberdare, its task was to inquire 'whether any alterations in the system of Poor Law relief are desirable in the case of persons whose destitution is occasioned by incapacity for work resulting from old age, or whether assistance could otherwise be afforded in those cases'. The members of that commission (of whom Charles Booth was one) had widely divergent views on what needed to be done. After two years it issued a report containing a wealth of evidence on the situation of the

[37] *National Review*, February 1892.

elderly poor. It suggested that pensions should be left to the friendly societies. It made no recommendations but agreed that the subject was extremely serious and needed to be examined further.

In 1896 a treasury committee chaired by Lord Rothschild was established to consider 'any contributory schemes that may be submitted to them for encouraging the industrial population, by State aid or otherwise, to make provision for old age, and to recommend any schemes, their cost, and how they may affect the Exchequer and local rates, their effect in promoting habits of thrift and self-reliance on the population, the influence on their prosperity and their possible cooperation'.

Neither the royal commission nor the treasury committee felt able to make recommendations. However, they did detail objections to those schemes that had been presented to them for consideration. The possibility of the 'undeserving' receiving aid was perceived as a serious problem and was of concern to both. It was generally believed that if the elderly were assured of a pension they would be disinclined to make provision for their own support and that there would be an 'injurious effect on wages'.

The treasury committee's other serious preoccupation was that the cost to ratepayers of any pension scheme should be as little as possible. Parliamentary select committee reports and subsequent bills reflected these anxieties and indicate that even those with a more liberal view on how the older members of society should be helped in a dignified way were careful to allay fears that the undeserving might benefit from a pension.

Outside parliament, the demand for an old age pension was growing. The intellectual case for pensions was developed by Charles Booth. In his addresses to campaign conferences organised by Francis Herbert Stead in 1898 and 1899, he outlined what he considered was the ideal condition in old age: physical comfort; independence; the power to give as well as to receive. He advocated that charity and Poor Law relief should be replaced by non-contributory pensions funded by general taxation. He pointed out that the old do not, except indirectly, share in general prosperity and that the poorest, in particular women, were not provided for by the friendly societies' insurance schemes.

It was the Christian social worker, Reverend Francis Herbert Stead who was instrumental in inspiring and initiating the organisation of a popular national movement to campaign around Booth's demands for old age pensions. Francis Herbert is much less known than his brother Will, the editor of the pioneering popular newspaper *Northern Star* and campaigner against child prostitution, who was drowned on the Titanic on his way to a peace conference. However, The Revd Stead's place in history is unquestionably as deserving.

Francis Herbert Stead was born in Howden, Tyneside in 1857. When he was 17 he was employed by his elder brother Will on the Northern Star as a junior reporter until he went to Glasgow University to study theology. After travelling in Europe, he took up a ministry in Leicester. He joined the Settlement movement which encouraged university graduates to live and work in deprived areas to alleviate the suffering of the poor, and in 1890 left Leicester to become the warden of the Robert Browning Settlement in York Street, Walworth, in South East London. This deprived borough had one of the highest proportion of paupers in the country. Under Stead's wardenship the Settlement organised a broad programme of recreational and educational activities for the poor people of Southwark. He was deeply affected by their suffering and he dedicated himself to the cause of abolishing pauperism until he died at Blackheath on January 14th 1928

Of his many charitable efforts, perhaps the most remarkable was the Settlement's 'goose club', the largest of its kind anywhere in the world. In 1908 for weekly contributions of less than two old pennies, its 10,383 members each received a goose, turkey or joint of beef and a large pack of groceries so that their families could have a good Christmas dinner and decent meals for a few days over the holiday.

Stead realised that charity itself was incapable of dealing with the needs of the elderly. He was of the opinion that state pensions were the only solution. From his friend William Pembert Reeves, the London Agent General of New Zealand, he had heard of the New Zealand government's decision to introduce a non-contributory old age pension of seven shillings per week for all at 65. Stead invited Reeves to speak about the New Zealand scheme at Browning Hall on 20 November 1898. (Charles Booth had also been asked to attend but was not able to do so.) Many trade unionists attended, and afterwards Mr A.E. Ball, later a Southwark councillor, suggested that it would be a shame not to follow up the interest and enthusiasm generated. As a result, the Revd Stead convened a further conference in the Browning Hall for 13 December 1898.

Stead chaired the December meeting at which Dr. Charles Booth was the main speaker. It was attended by 33 delegates mostly from Labour organisations, some from outside of London. They were George Barnes, his fellow members J. Kidd, and B. Wright of the Amalgamated Soc. Engineers; F.Chandler, Amalg. Soc. Carpenters and Joiners; J. Sansom, Nat. Union Gas Workers & Gen. Labourers; Cllr.Holmes, Nat.Hosiery & Dyers Fed.; J. Maddison, S. Masterson, Friendly Soc. of Iron founders; A. Wilkie, Ass.Shipwrights Soc.; John Lamb, Nat.Assoc.of Operative Plasterers; E.T. Mendell, London Cab Drivers Trade Union; W. Stevenson, United Builders' Union; J. Macpherson, Margaret Bondfield, Nat. Union of Shop Assistants; T. Chambers, Workers' Union; A. Collett, Nat. Union of Clerks; Emily Janes, Nat. Union of Women Workers; F. Newman, Smiths' & Fitters Union; D. Evans, Alliance & Furnishing Trade Assn.; J. MacDonald, London Trades Council; F. Sheppard, Bristol Trades Council; Cllr. Millington, Hull Trades Council; Cllr. Connellan, Leeds & District Trades Council; Fredk. Maddison, MP, Will Crooks, L.C.C.; Dr. G.W. Richards; Tom Bryan, MA; F. Butler; T. Holding; W. Wotman; Henrietta Jastrow, Berlin. Apologies were received from, Thomas Burt, M.P., John Burns, MP, and the Northumberland Miners Mutual Confident Association.

All in all, 266,314 workers were represented by trade union delegates, and a further 110,634 by trades councils.

It was resolved to convene further conferences, the first in Newcastle in January 1899, and then in Leeds, Manchester, Bristol, Glasgow and Birmingham. Clearly, there was a huge interest in the issue across many groups: hundreds of thousands of trade unionists, members of other Labour organisations, religious groups and friendly societies were represented at these meetings. The attendance at Birmingham was:

Delegates	Organisation	Members represented
175	Manchester Unity & other Orders of Odd Fellows	40,843
132	Ancient Order of Foresters	37,996
47	Cooperative societies	54,373
27	Trades councils	77,450
96	Trade unions	105,207
47	Other Economic Societies	23,121
10	Ancient Order of Buffaloes	4,612
17	Order of Druids	3,211
13	Order of Rechabites	737

Joseph Chamberlain had been invited to the Birmingham meeting, and while he did not attend, he indicated his interest and a few days later announced the appointment of a select committee on the Aged and Deserving Poor known as the 'Chaplin committee'.

Charles Booth addressed all the conferences organised by Stead, making a powerful social argument for the introduction of the pension. The Revd Francis Herbert Stead records Booth's speeches and the proceedings in his book *How Old Age Pensions Began to Be*.[38] Booth stirred audiences up and down the country with his convincing case for a universal, non-contributory old age pension. Arguing that everyone recognised the deplorable state of poverty in old age, of which pauperism was only one symptom, Booth pointed out that the old were industrially at a disadvantage and had no share in the general prosperity. Their ideal condition must provide comfort, independence and the 'power to give'. He stated that the maintenance of the old, and assistance to children, from savings, earnings, insurance, charity and poor relief was insufficient and undesirable. He ruled out contributory schemes because they would interfere with thrift agencies and pointed out that these schemes would not provide for all poor women, most of whom would be unable to contribute, and that they offered no benefit for the future generation.

[38] The Revd Francis Herbert Stead, *How Old Pensions Began to be*, Methuen & Co., London, 1909.

Booth stressed that the costs should be borne by general taxation and the benefits should be for all who claimed them. Against the objections usually expressed against non-contributory pensions he argued, as Sydney Webb had also previously argued,[39] that such a scheme would not check property accumulation, on the contrary it would encourage it. Moreover, it would not affect wage rates materially. Insurance and similar schemes would still be needed as would help from children, but, through the provision of a universal pension, charity would become less important and begging less fraudulent. Everywhere Charles Booth spoke, delegates supported the demand that the government should legislate for universal, non-contributory pensions enthusiastically.

After this series of conferences a group of delegates representing 37 trade unions and 2 trades councils met in January 1899 and formed the National Pensions Committee, linked to the National Committee of Organised Labour. The first chairman was J.V. Stevens, to be followed by George Barnes MP; the vice chair was G.D. Kelly MP; the position of honorary secretary was jointly taken by The Revd Francis Herbert Stead, and R. Waite; Frederick Rogers, the secretary of the Vellum Binders Union, was appointed to the paid post of organising secretary. He later became the first chair of the Labour Representation Committee (the forerunner of the Labour Party). Edward Cadbury acted as treasurer. The Executive committee members were Charles Booth, and many influential public figures and leaders of the trade union and Labour movement, including Albert Stanley, the miners' MP; Thomas Burt, MP; Federick Naddison; Francis Chandler; J.R. Clynes and Will Crooks.

On 9 May 1899 under Stead's leadership the National Pensions Committee called for a national campaign for universal non-contributory old age pensions at 65. In September the Trade Union Congress unanimously passed a resolution demanding a pension for all citizens of 60 years of age. A further demand followed in 1901from the Cooperative Societies.

However, it was not until 1906 that the next important advance along the road to the pension was made. In November that year, Stead and Frederick Rogers led 80 Labour and Liberal MPs to meet Sir Henry Campbell-Bannerman, leader of the Liberal Party, and Herbert Asquith.

---

[39] Sidney Webb, 'The Reform of the Poor Law', *The Contemporary Review*, July 1890, p.106.

They received private assurances that the Liberal ministry would undertake an Old Age Pensions bill.[40] However, this was not to come about for another year and a half.

---

[40] Bentley B. Gilbert describes the background to this meeting in *The Evolution of National Insurance in Great Britain*, Michael Joseph, 1966, reprinted Gregg Revivals, Aldershot, England, 1993.

Winning the argument

The maintenance of old age has hitherto been a private, not a public, charge. The proposal to alter this is more than an amendment of the Poor Law. It is a proposal to alter a fundamental principle of society. (T. Mackay)[41]

As a result of the campaign, and the nationwide support it received, things began to happen. The government had reopened its consideration of the case for a state pension by appointing the Select Committee on 'Improving the Condition of the Aged Deserving Poor' which reported to parliament on 26 July 1899.[42] The Chaplin committee (chaired by The Rt Hon. Henry Chaplin, a Unionist, President of the Board of Agriculture and the Local Government Board) was composed of a number of the leading political figures of the day.[43] They examined many witnesses who were mainly drawn from organisations involved with insurance and charity in order to review the existing insurance schemes and charities that aimed to assist the elderly who were unable to earn enough to live on, and who would otherwise rely entirely upon poor relief.

The committee accepted that the main reason advanced in support of a universal pension plan was that there were many cases of aged people for whom the perceived disgrace of being classified as paupers was unjustified. In the words of the committee's report, these were those

[41] T. Mackay, 'Subsidised Pensions for Old Age', *National Review*, March, p.351, 1892.

[42] Parliamentary Papers, Vol. 8, 1899.

[43] Committee members: Mr Anstruther, Mr Cripps, Lord Edmund Fitzmaurice a Liberal free trader and educationalist, Sir Walter Foster, Mr Hedderwick Scottish Liberal, Mr Samuel Hoare Conservative, Mr Lionel Holland, William Lecky, Unionist writer and representative for Trinity College Dublin, Evan Llewellyn landowner, Lloyd George, Mr A.K. Lloyd, Sir James Rankin the scientist, Mr William Redwood, Mr Woods, Sir Fortescue Flannery and Mr Davitt.

whose conduct and whole career has been blameless, industrious and deserving but find themselves, from no fault of their own, at the end of a long and meritorious life, with nothing but the workhouse or inadequate outdoor relief, as the refuge for their declining years.' They went so far as to state that the aid provided under the Poor Law was 'too often wholly inadequate to provide for the reasonable comfort and even the barest necessities of the poor'.

Mr Knollys, the chief general inspector of the Local Government Board testified that, as a rule, outdoor relief was between two shillings and sixpence and three shillings a week. Mr Baldwyn Fleming, a senior inspector said that 'I think that to try to make old people live on two shillings and sixpence and a loaf for a week is intensely cruel.' The committee indicated in their report that they desired to provide adequately for these old people and thought that this could be done 'without any undue discouragement either to thrift or the self-respecting efforts which many of the poor are making now to secure provision for themselves in their old age'.

Apart from the evidence which was available to them from the earlier Aberdare and Rothchild committees, the Chaplin committee also sought views of experts on existing private insurance and pension schemes. For this, they relied upon the opinions and experience of the friendly and benefit societies, who viewed any move to create a state pension scheme as a threat to their business. Many were already quite well established and were increasing in number and scope. Indeed, their total membership in 1898 was over four million. These private insurance schemes relied upon building up funds to support pension payments: their plans offered future pensions to young people when they became elderly. As a result, they were unable to address the present needs of old people, as to do this would necessitate immediate funding. Accumulating adequate funds to generate the income required to pay out the pensions would take time. Many years would have to elapse from the date of receipt of the initial premium before they could provide for any appreciable number of persons. The oldest established society at that time appeared to have been in existence for only 24 years.

The inability of the friendly societies to address the immediate problem of providing for existing, as against future, old people was illustrated by

Sir John Dorrington. He testified that a benefit society, with which he was connected, could (if rates of interest and enrolment rate held) eventually provide sick benefits and an annuity of five shillings per week at the age of 65 to a man, 'providing he had paid contributions of one penny per day from the age of 25'. He said that this contribution could be afforded by agricultural workers. Clearly, this society was offering nothing to assist the current population of older people, as 40 years would have to elapse before such a scheme could be effective.

James Davy, a general inspector of the Local Government Board, who had gone to Denmark to study their scheme, reported his findings. He told the committee that the Danish state pension scheme had been in operation since 1891 and that on reaching 60, Danes could apply to the Communal Authority for a pension if they were native born. There were also other requirements: they had to be without means and practically destitute; not have been involved with dishonourable transactions; have brought poverty upon themselves by, for example, extravagance; and not have received Poor Law relief for 10 years prior to their application. Pensions were fixed at 'what is necessary to supplement a man's means to enable him to live'. A head of a family received between two shillings and three shillings and fourpence per week depending upon where they resided. If in the country, a provincial town or Copenhagen, single persons received between one and four pence and two shillings and eightpence. The state and local community contributed equally to the costs. The authorities could withdraw the pension from the recipient in certain cases of abuse, but this seldom occurred. The main difference between the Danish pension scheme and English Poor Law outdoor relief was that the Danish pension scheme was claimed as a right and carried no civil disqualifications.

Sir Henry Longley, the chief UK charity commissioner, told the committee that in recent years his commission had established an old age pension scheme. In 1898 a total income of £611,464 was derived from endowed charities. This was devoted to pensions and almshouses. A further £327,625 was provided to Dole charities. 'Charity pensioners" had to be poor, good characters, provident and not have received Poor Law relief for five years but who now found that they were unable to maintain themselves because of old age, ill-health, accidental injury or infirmity. There were no fixed age limits. Pensions were between five and ten shillings per week. The trustees decided who was entitled to benefit.

Mr Munro, the clerk of Wells and Camden Charity, noted that his charity required candidates for pensions to have an income of at least five shillings weekly. Along with saving bank deposits, etc., this was taken as proof of thrift

Twenty-two other pension charities gave evidence to the 1899 committee. All required claimants to have good characters. Most accepted that if the claimant had not been in receipt of Poor Law relief, this would be accepted as evidence of thrift, which prevailed as an essential condition to be fulfilled by would-be pensioners.

The Chaplin committee concluded that it was practicable to create a workable system of old age pensions for the United Kingdom. However, schemes for universal pensions without regard to merit and thrifts were outside the 1899 committee's terms of reference. They rejected schemes requiring compulsory contributions out of earnings from an early age, along the lines of the system in Germany, because they thought these would be opposed by the very class of people they were aiming to help and that anyway benefits would be deferred for many years.

In view of these conclusions it would be reasonable to have expected that the committee would have decided to go along with a proposal to grant pensions to all citizens over 65 years of age with income less than ten shillings per week providing they were not receiving Poor Law relief and had not been convicted of a criminal offence for 10 years prior to their pension claim. Nonetheless, the committee rejected the idea. The reason given was that if these categories were included, the resulting numbers of eligible pensioners would be so large that the cost of any scheme would be extremely high. The qualifications that the committee formulated were mainly conceived with the objective of reducing the number of possible claimants and thus the projected cost. They recommended that pensions should only be available to British subjects of 65 years of age who had not received poor relief, other than medical aid, for 20 years prior to claiming, and who during this period had not been sentenced to imprisonment, without the option of a fine. The claimants must have endeavoured to provide for themselves and their dependants, and be residents in one of the pension authorities which, the committee proposed, should be established in each union. These authorities would be composed of members of the Board of Guardians. They further advised that claimants' other income should not exceed ten shillings weekly.

The pension recommended was between five and seven shillings weekly, at the discretion of the pension authority committee. The actual pension level would be assessed according to the cost of living in the area. It should be paid weekly at a post office and be awarded for not less than three years, but it could be withdrawn at any time at the discretion of the pension committee. The committee recommended that applications for pensions should be made on a form signed before a justice of the peace without fee. Costs of the scheme would be borne by the Common Fund of the Union and half of the total costs would be put into the Common Fund by the government.

Although these recommendations would not meet the real needs of the time when large numbers of destitute and starving people were roaming the streets, what *is* noteworthy is that the principle of entitling the aged in need to a non-contributory pension by right, an almost revolutionary measure, had been conceded by the 1899 committee. It implied that the aged poor and destitute were products of society and therefore were society's responsibility and had a right to sustenance for their remaining years. It was also notable that the right to a pension was recommended to be processed outside the existing framework in use for administrating Poor Law relief and that it should be paid out by the post office. This represented a very early challenge by government to the administrative role of the strongly established Boards of Guardians.

The Boer War (1899–1902), which was to cost the country £250 million, provided an excuse for delaying parliamentary action on the committee's recommendations. However, the campaigns for old age pensions led by the National Pensions Committee and the National Committee of Organised Labour on Old Age Pensions were to continue outside parliament. Moreover, the 1899 committee report was to inspire the proposals of a number of unsuccessful bills in the nine years preceding the bill that finally resulted in the first State Old Age Pensions Act of 1908. The wording and provisions of these bills demonstrate some reluctance to antagonise private business, but, more importantly, the prejudices of those times against the poor and the acute fear of 'helping the undeserving'. Some of these prejudices found their way into the final legislation passed in 1908 and, as will be seen from the following summary, regrettably surface today.

The 1901 Bill No. 23 was clearly aimed to reassure the friendly societies that their interests would not be adversely affected by a national pension scheme. It moved that persons of 25 years of age, who insured with a friendly society against sickness with rights of 13 weeks of benefits of seven shillings and sixpence weekly for a man and five shillings weekly for a woman, should be entitled to a pension of five shillings per week from the county council at the age of 65. The exceptions were those on poor relief or imprisoned, and those in regular employment waged at five shillings weekly or with an income of £40 per year. Women and widows were included. At 65, claims for a pension from those who had been in friendly societies for five years immediately prior to 1901 would be accepted providing other qualifications were met. Such pensions would cease on imprisonment or would be paid to the guardians if the pensioner was in the workhouse. Two-thirds of the funding should be by the county council via a parliamentary fund and one-third from county council rates.

Bill No. 61 was aimed specifically to pension deserving and thrifty people without hard and fast rules on what other income would be permitted. There was the usual disqualification if the claimant was receiving poor relief because this was always regarded as stemming only from the person's neglect to have saved for rainy days. A claimant's possible lack of thrift and merit would be decided by a local committee. No pension was to be granted if imprisonment had occurred during the 15 years prior to claiming and there were to be no drunkenness convictions for the previous 10 years. Funding was to be from a special rate.

Both bills underlined that receipt of poor relief was a reason for refusing a pension. This demonstrated the general view held by parliament that, over 55 years of age, poverty was due to moral weakness, and to discourage this it was justifiable to deny such people the right to a pension. Their punishment was to be condemned to pauperism.

Bill No. 62 was significant because it partly broke away from this concept. For the first time, parliament seemed to appreciate that receipt of poor relief was not automatically an indication of laziness and lack of thrift. It proposed that the receipt of poor relief should be permitted if it was received due to illness or widowhood. It also introduced cover for pensioner's widows and dependent children.

These 1900, albeit unsuccessful, bills began to show that a more sympathetic attitude was developing to providing for the aged.

In 1901 five more unsuccessful bills were put down. For the first time, a pension book was mentioned although most parliamentarians regarded the Guardians, who were a strong force and were jealous of their authority, as the most appropriate channel for the administration of any eventual pension plan.

Bill No. 20 made some significant recommendations. It wanted the qualification to entitlement to include British residency for 30 years, clean criminal records for the immediately preceding 10 years, and that poor relief should not have been received since the age of 21 for a continuous period of more than two years. Five shillings per week was to be paid to the pensioner at a Money Order Office on production of a pension book and a representative would be permitted to collect the pension on behalf of an ill person unable to attend. In deference to the establishment's dread of pensioning a law breaker or drunkard, the bill stated that the pension should be forfeited if the pensioner was convicted to three months, or more, imprisonment, or, if a court found the pensioner guilty of drunkenness more than twice in 12 months. It was proposed that pensions should be funded by the government; two-thirds of the costs were to be from Consolidated UK Fund and one-third from the Exchequer.

Bill No. 30 aimed to restore civil rights to qualified pensioners presently on poor relief by involving Guardians to draw up a list of deserving pensioners. No doubt, this was with a view to allaying their fears that their role in managing the poor would weaken.

Bill No. 57 proposed to relax slightly the qualifications listed in Bill No. 20 by allowing discretion to be exercised, but limited other income to £40 yearly. This bill mentions women specifically and widows, on reaching 65, were to receive their deceased husbands' pensions and the right to continue their insurance contributions. Funding again was to be from the county council, two-thirds from monies transferred from parliament, the rest from county council rates.

Bill No. 110 aimed to ensure that HM Forces personnel were also entitled to claim for pensions.

The 1901 bills observed widows' needs and further attempted to take the funding and administration of pensions further away from the control of the charities and Guardians.

The concept of universal pensions continued to gain wider acceptance during the following year. In 1902 a further two bills (Nos 9 and 15) were published. These did not come up with greatly different or new ideas. However, a reduction in the level of other income permitted before pension rights were affected. It was decreased from £40 to £26 yearly. In addition, the requirement for a residential qualification was raised.

The Chaplin Select committee met in 1903. This made recommendations that were incorporated in a significant bill tabled that year, which proposed that the local authorities join with the Board of Guardians and the friendly societies in creating the Pension Authority Committee. The object of this was to assure them they would influence who would be awarded a pension, and that they would be involved with in the administering of the system.

It proposed that the state's funding of pensions should be limited to a maximum annual contribution of £2 million and that there should be an additional contribution from local rates of a sum up to the amount of the state's contribution. A means-test was suggested to ensure that claimants really were in need. This would take into account the value of any property owned by the claimant as well as any current income. The property valued would include furniture and chattels. If the means-test revealed that these could be sold and converted into an annuity providing £30 annually, the pension claim would fail although this was unlikely unless the claimant owned a house or land.

The recommendations of the 1899 and 1903 Select committees were incorporated in seven later bills published in 1904, 1905 1906 and 1907. The only remarkable proposal contained was in the 1906 Bill No. 28. This proposed a qualification that, not only pensioners should be British, but that they should be of European descent. This, happily, was not included in any subsequent bill. It was also moved that pension claims should be made on a form countersigned by two ratepayers and adjudicated by the Registrar of Births, Deaths and Marriages.

Parliamentary opinion was clearly that local authorities were essential in the administration of pensions, that the main funding should be from the Treasury and that payment should be through the Post Office.

Much of the traditionally harsh and patronising attitude to the poor was still evident in all the bills tabled between 1899 and 1907. They stressed that pensioners were to have clean criminal records and were to have never been convicted of serious drunkenness. Further, claimants had to be able to prove that they had always been hardworking and thrifty. The 'right' to a pension was conditional upon proof of need and the threat of destitution. Therefore, a means-test would be necessary to evaluate any current income received by the claimant, and the value of any property owned, including its potential to provide an income if sold. Although unsuccessful, these bills and the debates around them marked real progress towards the very first Old Age Pensions Act of 1908.

The 'Lord George'

'We put it forward as incomplete; it is a beginning and only a beginning.' (Lloyd George)

The National Pensions Committee meeting at the Browning Tavern in Southwark on 21 July 1907, called attention to the growing dissatisfaction with the government's delay in delivering its promises to introduce an old age pension. It was pointed out that this was the principal reason for the defeat of the previous government's candidates in the recent by-elections in Jarrow and Colne Valley where Labour candidates Pete Curran and Victor Grayson, who were in favour of the urgent introduction of old age pensions, had been returned. The committee anticipated similar results in other constituencies unless there was official assurance that the measures to provide pensions for all in their old age would be taken in the next parliamentary year.

The campaign was stepped up. The Committee, together with Labour organisations and the Trade Union Congress[44] organised public meetings throughout the country. The Labour Representation Committee and Labour MPs declared their active support and 560 petitions with 799,750 signatures were presented to parliament by F. Jowett (MP for Bradford). In reply to an article in the *Westminster Gazette* expressing the view that the state would not pay a pension to all old people regardless of means and character, George Bernard Shaw wrote 'There must be no doubt that Old Age pensions will inevitably come at 65 ... all this nonsense about deserving cases ... must be dropped'.

On behalf of the committee, The Revd Stead wrote a letter, which he referred to as a manifesto, setting out the position to all members of the

---

[44] D. Goodman, *No Thanks to Lloyd George*, Third Age Press, 1998.

cabinet and leaders of the opposition and this no doubt had considerable effect on the government's position leading up to the introduction of the bill in 1908. Clearly, support for the pension had become a force that would win the day.

In setting out the financial situation surrounding the consideration of introducing the old age pension, Herbert Asquith indicated that income tax at ninepence in the pound had brought in an additional £750,000, and a very healthy budget surplus of nearly £5 million was expected. However, only £1.2 million were to be allocated that year for pensions – less than half of that originally promised. A five-shilling pension was generally agreed. The income limit at £26 per year was proposed and the age of entitlement was to be 'at first' 70. Importantly, the character test for entitlement was to be dropped. The first reading of the bill was on 28 May, 1908, the second on 15 and 16 June.[45]

The government argued that because cost was of paramount importance, the qualifying age must be 70. The majority of members accepted the government's case, fearing perhaps that the cost of the proposed pension scheme threatened the implementation of the bill most seriously. In the background there was an idea that in order to phase in the cost burden, the age could be lowered in stages from 70 to 65. This had been mooted in Bill No. 17, unsuccessfully tabled the year before. That bill had proposed the gradual lowering of the qualifying age from 75 in 1908, to 70 in 1909 and finally to 65 in 1910. Most members spoke in favour of a qualifying age of 65 years, not 70, but cost considerations prevailed and the proposal to make the pension age 70 years finally won the day.

The non-contributory basis of the scheme was supported by the majority because of the obvious inability of most workers to contribute. The government's assessment of the average wage as being twenty-four shillings and ninepence was disputed by Mr O'Grady (Leeds East) who considered eighteen shillings was the correct figure. In support, Mr Burt (Morpeth) said that one-third of English workers earned less than twenty shillings and Mr Flynn (Cork) said Irish agricultural workers were receiving between nine and twelve shillings weekly (with a shilling less in winter). These workers certainly couldn't have afforded to contribute towards a pension scheme. Mr Mond, MP for Chester quoted Bismarck,

---

[45] Parliamentary Debates (*Hansard*) 1908, Fourth Series, Vols 190 and 191.

'That the veterans of labour are entitled to a pension as much as the veterans of war'; and Lloyd George noted that 'A workman who has contributed health and strength, vigour and skill, to the creation of wealth by which taxation is borne has made his contribution already to the fund which is to give him a pension when he is no longer fit to create that wealth'.

The level of the pension was to have some relationship to average wages. Many members had taken the view that the proposed five shillings a week, approximating to between 20 per cent and 25 per cent of the average wage, was hardly adequate for an old person to live on. This was hardly surprising, considering that over a hundred years previously, the scale established at Speenhamland, Berkshire, which was widely used as a basis for calculating doles, set relief for a single man at three shillings weekly.[46] The cost to the Treasury of a pension of five shillings per week to those qualifying at 70 was estimated to be in the region of £7,500,000 a year (the actual cost in 1909, the first year, was £2,026,395 and in 1910, when the scheme had become fully established, £8,468,128).[47]

There were many restrictions. Claimants were disqualified if they were in receipt of poor relief unless for dependants' funeral expenses, medical assistance, maintenance in a hospital, asylum etc. No pension would be granted if, given ability and opportunity, there had been habitual failure to work which had caused the needs of the claimant or dependants not to have been met. This condition was waived if, between the age of 50 and 60, the claimant had paid contributions continually into friendly or benefit societies to insure against old age, sickness or unemployment. Conviction of a criminal offence resulting in imprisonment without the option of a fine would disqualify a pensioner from receiving payment for the period of imprisonment and for a further ten years after release. A pensioner liable, through the court, to be detained under the Inebriates Act of 1898 also would lose the pension whilst detained and, at the court's discretion, for up to ten years after release.

The full pension of five shillings weekly was to be paid if other annual income was not more than £21. Couples living together in the same house

---

[46] M. Neuman, The Speenhamland County, Poverty and the Poor Laws in Berkshire 1782–1834, Garland Publishing Inc. New York and London, 1982.

[47] Report of the 1919 Departmental Committee on Old Age Pensions.

would each receive three shillings and ninepence weekly instead of the five shillings, if they satisfied other conditions of entitlement.

A means-test was applied to take into account other income, value or advantages that could be gained from ownership of property. The test took into account both the yearly income that could be expected to be derived from the value of property owned and, if it were to be sold, invested or put to profitable use. The value of any benefit or privilege would also be taken into account. A couple's other means would be considered to benefit one by at least half the joint total. The basic single pension of five shillings was reduced on a sliding scale if other annual income was between £21. and £31 and ten shillings. So, for every shilling the weekly income exceeded eight shillings and one penny, one shilling was deducted from the basic five shillings. If other income exceeded twelve shillings and one penny per week then no pension was paid. In effect the old age pension was the old age pension for the poor.

The authority and adjudication of the pension scheme would reside in a Local Pensions Committee appointed for each borough and urban district having a population of at least 20,000 by the borough, district or county council. The central authority was the Local Government Board and pension officers were appointed by the Treasury. The claim for a pension was to be simple and in writing. All funding was borne by the state.

Representing the National Pensions Committee, Frederick Maddison welcomed the bill and paid particular tribute to Charles Booth for his part in the campaign that led to the bill, and after a 'wrecking amendment' only gained the support of 29 members the second reading was carried without a division. The great step had been taken. Old age pensions, although means-tested, were at last established. On reaching 70, poor people could collect their 'Lord George' (or should it have been known as the 'Francis Herbert Stead'?) at the post office for the first time on 1 January, 1909. Up to 31 March 1909, 837,831 claims for the old age pension were received. Of these, 102,100 were rejected. On 31 March 1909, 647,494 received the pension of whom 582,565 pensioners received the full five shillings.[48]

Since the 1899 Select committee's report, public opinion had progressed, but it had not changed enough to remove the insistence on 'proof of

[48] Fifty-second Report of the Commissioners of H.M. Inland Revenue.

need', i.e a means-test, and that the pensioner should be moral and 'deserving'. Both of these 'principles' were deeply rooted in the culture of the Poor Law and the workhouse. Even though those who receive it today have made contributions throughout their working life, the old age pension is still associated with charity. The struggle for dignity in old age will not be won until this is eradicated.

Nevertheless, the first British state old age pension scheme was a move a long way from Poor Law provision by the Board of Guardians. Apart from detailed amendments made in 1911, the scheme became well established. Five years later, in recognition of the increased cost of living, an additional allowance of two shillings and sixpence per week was made. In 1910, the second year of the 1908 Act, 699,352 older men and women of 70 and over received pensions; by 1919 that number had risen to 920,198 and the cost had more than doubled from £8,468,128 to £17,728,000.

Living on the pension

The introduction of the pension reduced the number of elderly paupers, but, in spite of the granting in 1916 of an extra two shillings and sixpence per week in recognition of the increasing cost of living,. with an income of only between seven and six and thirteen shillings per week, many found it very hard to live outside of the workhouse.

In 1919 a Departmental Committee on Old Age Pensions was appointed 'to consider and report what alterations, if any, as regard rates of pension or qualification should be made in the existing statutory scheme of Old Age Pensions'.[49] The committee took evidence over a period of 27 days from 52 persons representing Customs and Excise, Ministry of Health, pension administrators, private companies, friendly societies, trade unions and two old age pensioners. The extent to which this improved the lot of pensioners can be judged by considering a typical budget of a widow pensioner living alone in Hampstead, London who provided evidence to the committee:[50]

---

[49] Departmental Committee on Old Age Pensions 1919. Members: Sir W. Ryland; D. Adkins; MP (Chairman); Sir Henry A. Robinson, Vice-President Local Board for Ireland; Sir Arthur J. Tedder Ex-Customs & Excise; Sir Alfred W. Watson, Government Actuary; Sir Theodore G. Chambers, Controller, National War Savings Committee; Ewan F. Macpherson, Legal member, Local Government Board Scotland; Lt Colonel Nathan Raw, MP; Mr W.A. Appleton, Secretary General, Federation of Trade Unions; Mr H.J. Comyns, Local Government Board; Joseph Devlin, MP; Mr J.H. Dunford High Chief Ranger of the Ancient Order of Foresters; Major J.G. Jameson, MP; Miss M. Cecile Matheson; Arnold Rowntree, MP; Mr G.R. Thorne, MP; Stephen Walsh MP; Mrs H.J. Baker and Mr Henry Woodhall.

[50] Evidence to 1919 Departmental Committee on Old Age Pensions by Mrs Jane Stuart, Pensions Officer for Marylebone and Hampstead; *Parliamentary Papers*, Vol. 27, 1919.

Income	s	d	Gen. expenses	s	d	Food	s	d
Pension + allowance	7.	6	Rent	3.	0	Meat & veg.	2.	1
Benefit society	3.	0	Coal	1.	4	Bread & marg.		$10\frac{1}{2}$
Earnings (needlework)	3.	6	Oil		4	Bacon & eggs	1.	$5\frac{1}{2}$
Total	**14.**	**0**	Gas		6	Tea & sugar	1.	$0\frac{1}{2}$
			Insurance		2	Milk	1.	1
			Soap		4	Fish		$2\frac{1}{2}$
			Sundries		2	Jam	1.	5
			Total	**5.10**		**Total**	**8.**	**2**

Nothing was left for clothes or shoe repairs.

Mrs Caroline Thompson, a Birmingham lady of 73, also gave evidence to the 1919 committee. Her husband had been an invalid for14 years before he died in 1917. Mrs Thompson had worked for 53 years at Baker and Fennimore (a company still in business in 2006 manufacturing precision presswork, with 100 employees). Her last job there, from which she retired, was as a pen-nib slitter at nine shillings per week. She did not receive any pension from her ex-employer.

Mrs Thompson lived alone in one room and had to manage on nine shillings sixpence per week. This was made up by five shillings state pension plus two shillings sixpence additional allowance and a further two shillings from the local charitable settlement. Out of this, three shillings went on rent. She told the commission that her main concern was to keep her fire going through the night because 'I have to get in and out of bed so much'. Coal consequently cost her up to one shilling elevenpence each week. Her weekly diet typically consisted of 4 ounces of bacon, potatoes, bread and butter, jam, tea, and tinned milk. In return for washing up and sewing for friends she received a little cake, some food and, from time to time, used clothing. Mrs Thompson paid threepence per week burial money to The Prudential.

Another witness interviewed by the commission was Mrs Elizabeth Lorton who was 72 years old. Her husband had died 36 years earlier. She had been employed as a button carder in Birmingham until she was 70, working from eight o'clock in the morning to seven in the evening on week days, and on Saturdays from eight to one. Her pay was eight or nine shillings per week. On this wage, she had little opportunity to save for her old age. She told the committee that in addition to seven and sixpence pension she received two shillings from subletting a room in her back-to-back house in Summer Lane. She also earned about four or five shillings from part-time work for the police. This consisted of sitting at night with prisoners who were considered likely to commit suicide. She was paid 'tuppence ha'penny' per hour, but this work was not regularly available. Mrs Lorton was limited in the amount of washing she could take in due to having had a stroke. She paid four shillings and sixpence rent and spent two shillings and sixpence a week for a hundredweight of coal and two pennyworth of slack to make it go further. Firewood and lamp oil accounted for another two shillings per week. This left her with eight or nine shillings for food and clothing. Elizabeth Lorton mended her own shoes.

These ladies were typical of the widows struggling to maintain a respectable but modest life in the years that followed the First World War. They made every effort to be independent but were in fact, even with the old age pension, likely to spend their last years on public assistance and charity.

From the evidence and statements of the witnesses, it became patently clear that the pension was quite inadequate to provide a decent home and dignified life at the most modest level for the elderly who were unable to continue in employment.

The main recommendations of the committee were that:
1 Pensions should be increased and additional cost of living allowance absorbed. The new consolidated rate should be ten shillings per week.
2 That the means-test be abandoned.
3 That, whilst leaving the age of qualification at 70, something should be done to ensure that provision be made for those, especially women, younger than 70 by means of national insurance.
4 That when a pensioner is admitted through illness to the workhouse, the pension shall still be paid for three months but, as far as possible, it should be seen to be used for dependants or maintenance of the pensioner's private home.

5 The 10-year disqualification for released criminals should be abolished except for 'habitual inebriates'. The 'failure to work' disqualification should also be dropped.

The 1919 committee had reaffirmed the right to a universal non-contributory pension at 70 and aimed to remove more of the patronising aspects of the conditions of qualification, including the means-test.

The economic slump of the 1920s brought huge rises in unemployment, and millions lived in poverty. The first Labour government fell in 1925; working-class militancy was increasing. The establishment was shaken. The government needed to mollify the opposition but at the same time it had to grapple with the problem of keeping the economy afloat and maintaining its position in the financial world. In addition, taxation was to be kept as low as possible.

In 1925, in an attempt to deal with the growing dissatisfaction of the working people, Neville Chamberlain put forward a National Contributory Insurance plan for pensions, sickness and unemployment. This was a brilliant move, for not only did it assist the deprived, but could be expected to do so with very little cost to the Exchequer. It entailed no serious increase in taxation. The potential beneficiaries paid through their contributions to a national insurance scheme. As a result, workers were assured of subsistence for themselves and their families even if thrown out of work before reaching pensionable age. The other contributor, the employer, felt politically more secure and could in most cases recoup costs in wage and price determinations. Chamberlain's bill was passed. In January 1926, the year of the General Strike, when poor relief was doled out to 2,440,629 people, 187,143 received 'domiciliary relief' costing on average seven shillings and fourpence weekly. The year's total expenditure was £49.5 million.[51]

Contributory national insurance brought a significant improvement to the lives of older people. The existing pension at 70 was increased to ten shillings per week and the newly insured employed would receive the pension five years earlier. Pensioners' widows would receive the pension on reaching 60 years. It meant that all insured people received pensions at 65 without means-testing. At last the pension was a universal right for

---

[51] Annual Report of the Ministry of Health, HMSO, London, 1927.

all contributors and the age of qualification had become the one proposed 30 years previously. For workers, the pension was no longer charity as it had been modified to accommodate a contributory scheme. Further improvements followed. In 1929 widows of 55 became pensioners and in 1930 a further Act legislated that women at 60, insured independently or through their husband's contributions, joined men at 65 in having the right to a pension.

However, the pension of ten shillings per week was, in real terms, about one-third less than the five shillings received in 1914, hardly enough to provide basic needs. Moreover, those unable to contribute to the national insurance scheme remained on poor relief, and that year it was granted to 229,102 people over 70, who were 2.5 times more likely to rely on public assistance than the rest of the population. Their reliance on indoor poor medical relief was 7.5 times greater. In 1871 the annual Poor Law cost of sustaining paupers had cost £8,700,403 (about £9. 8s.11d.per head). By 1906 it had risen to £14,685,938 (£14.13s.11d.),[52] an increase of 55 per cent.

In 1908 the old age pension had replaced poor relief for the over 70s, but unemployed able-bodied paupers still relied upon poor relief. To reduce the cost incurred, unemployment obviously needed to be reduced. William Beveridge, who, 30 years later, influenced the establishment of the welfare state, proposed setting up labour exchanges, and in 1909, after four years work, the Royal Commission on the Poor Law recommended their establishment. Originally, in 1910, these were to help the unemployed to find work, but they laid the basis for the introduction of unemployment insurance in 1913.

Progress was being made on the road from the Poor Laws. The working man and woman were emerging from the threat of pauperism.

---

[52] J.R.S.S. Hamilton, *Statistical Survey*, 1910.

The Welfare State

The Second World War was not limited to the battlefields. Millions of ordinary people in occupied countries fought in the resistance or supported those who did. In Britain all men and women who were not serving in the armed forces were mobilised. 'Home-front' manufacturing and agriculture were harnessed to the war effort – production of food, arms, planes and tanks for the Forces became the overriding national objective. Industry, whilst remaining in private ownership, was subjected to controls. Trade unions and Labour, traditional opponents of fascism, undoubtedly inspired by the heroic defence of the Soviet Union, cooperated with employers to maximise production. Men and women, many of whom, in the pre-war years, had never had opportunities to develop their talents and skills, were trained and conscripted to work in factories and on the land, many being directed to live in hostels miles from home. The togetherness and sense of purpose of the trenches experienced in the First World War extended to a far greater part of the population than in any previous conflict.

The British people saw how the nation's resources could be mobilised to meet the country's needs and were convinced could lay the basis for a better and fairer society. In 1945 victory was followed by the election of a Labour government with a huge majority and the first steps were made to establish a welfare state.

Before the Second World War poverty had been regarded as the condition in which human survival was threatened, in other words, 'destitution'. After the war poverty was seen as the condition of existing significantly below the average standard of living. This implied that its relief depended more on social justice than charity. It gave force to the concept that society has a duty not only to keep the poor alive and off the streets but to provide a decent life for everyone. There was a recognition that opportunities and rewards for some were absent, not due purely to personal failure, but as a result of society's failures. The idea that society, rather than the individual, is responsible for the existence of poverty, is one of great significance. The Victorians had been most reluctant to accept such a revolutionary concept.

Poverty of older people was, therefore, a major concern of post-war Britain. One essential part of the foundation of a new welfare state that would address this issue had already been laid. This was the landmark *Social Insurance and Allied Services Report*, published in 1942. (The Social Insurance and Allied Services committee was chaired by Sir William Beveridge and the report was to become widely known as the Beveridge report.) The popular acceptance of this report reflected clearly the national determination to deal with, not only with poverty, but, to leave behind the insecure times of the past and to create a healthier and more just society.

The Beveridge report examined how the government could meet the needs of those unable to provide for themselves due to unemployment, incapacity or age. It represented all sections of government responsible for social services.[53] Its terms of reference were to survey all existing national schemes and to make recommendations based upon that survey. The committee believed that social security should be achieved through cooperation between the state and the individual. It recognised that, whilst its prime objective was to eliminate want, the other 'giants' – disease, ignorance, squalor and idleness – had also to be defeated by the creation of a welfare state.

The report pointed to causes of poverty – causes which had long been appreciated by social reformers. It indicated that before the war 75 per cent to 83 per cent of those below subsistence were there not due to laziness or lack of effort but due to the loss of earning power. The remainder were in want mainly due to their earnings being inadequate to

---

[53] Command Report *'Social Insurance & Allied Services'*, Parliamentary Papers, 1942–43, Vol. 6. Committee members: Sir William Beveridge (Chairman); R.R. Bannatyre, Home Office; P.Y. Blundun, Min. Lab. & Nat. Service; Miss M.S. Cox OBE, Min. Pensions; Sir George Epps KBE CB, Gvt Actuary; R. Hamilton Farrell, Min. Health; E. Hale CB, Treasury; Mrs M.A. Hamilton, Reconstruction Secretariat; A.W. McKenzie, Board of Customs & Excise; Sir George Reid KBE CB, Assistance Board; Miss M. Ritson CBE, Dept Health Scotland; B.K. White, Registry of Friendly Socs. & Office of Ind. Assurance Commissioner; D.N. Chester (Secretary).

support dependants or save for rainy days. Beveridge considered that the total national income was sufficient to abolish want, and recommended that there should be a redistribution that would take into account family need. The way to do this, he suggested, was through social insurance. Given the prevailing system for the distribution of wealth, and reluctance to rely on high taxation to provide social needs, he considered it was important to maintain high levels of employment, and this has indeed remained the declared aim of all post-war governments.

The report recommended that retirement pensions should be provided without means-testing or upper-income limitation, and paid as of right to women and men by virtue of their contributions to a national insurance. The qualifying ages should be 60 for women and 65 for men. A weekly pension of twenty-three shillings (£1.15) for a single person and forty shillings (£2.00) for a couple were considered appropriate levels. These were based upon an assumed increase in the cost of living on that of 1938. The actual pensions paid under the new scheme in 1948 were £1.30 for the single pensioner and £2.10 for a couple, just 13 per cent and 5 per cent respectively above those suggested by Beveridge. The cost had been estimated to be £697 million, the bulk of which was to be covered by weekly contributions of four shillings and threepence (21.3p) per worker plus an additional three shillings and threepence (16.3p) from the employer.

The national insurance basic state pension, therefore, retained the contributory basis originally introduced by Joseph Chamberlain 42 years earlier. It was not to be a charitable handout. The contributions from employees and employers are paid into the national insurance fund which pays out the pensions. It is a 'Pay as You Go' system that does not rely upon returns from invested contributions. Today, employees pay contributions of about 11 per cent of their wages above a lower and below a higher level (this is about the same as that levied by similar schemes in other parts of Europe). Employers pay 12 per cent of their wages bill (much less than in Europe; in France for example, employers pay approximately 40 per cent).

Today, to qualify for the full basic state retirement pension, men must have a record of 44 years of contributions, women 39 years rising during the years 2010 to 2020, to 44 as their state pension age rises from 60 to 65.

Those who did not manage to work or earn enough to contribute for the period that carries entitlement to a full pension, receive a proportionally lower basic pension.

The amount collected each year by the national insurance fund has never been sufficient to accrue a balance which, if invested, would yield a return from which pensions could be paid. Indeed, that has never been its objective. The fund is a 'kitty'. The funds in this 'kitty' must always 'cover' at least 16 weeks' outgoings. This balance is placed in consolidated government stock yielding a very modest return. The fund is operated so that it meets its commitments without any substantial grants from the Treasury. Contributions in excess of expenditure are carried forward from one year to the next (see Appendix, Table 1).

Whether the state can afford to increase pensions or maintain the existing levels depends upon what's in the 'kitty'. It can be enlarged by increasing contributions or making Treasury grants. Currently, present pensions are more than met by contributions. Increasing the pension calls for raising the contributions, or adding to the national insurance fund from other sources, for example, Treasury grants. The substantial surplus in the fund which has been rising steadily, could also be used.

The Committee of Public Accounts' Fiftieth National Insurance Fund account report states that the Department's view is that the fund 'is naturally buoyant, and, ... should no longer require subsidies, and that there was no need to raise contribution levels'. Since then, the surplus in the fund has topped £35 billion. It has to remain in the National Insurance Fund but the government can borrow from it, at a very favourable rate, to finance expenditure of no direct benefit to the national insurance fund contributors. The surplus is on track to increase year by year, giving rise to a widely held view that, instead of providing loans to government, it should be used to increase the basic pension.

From 1948 to 1976 the basic state pension kept pace with inflation and the cost of basics as measured by the Retail Price Index. This link was considered necessary to ensure that the absolute living standard of the pensioner remained stable. But as the economy develops and wages rise more than inflation, this indexing does nothing to prevent the gap increasing between the retired and those in paid work whose wages increase at a higher rate.

The argument that retirement pensions should relate to the Gross Domestic Product and thus to the general prosperity of the nation is powerful. The rational for this lies in the recognition of the role of the past generation in laying the basis for present prosperity. The premise that, as prosperity grows, so should the living standard of the pensioner, although not incorporated in the official review procedure which only recognises inflation, has largely been accepted in practice. Had it not done so, pensioners would today be enduring the same standard of living experienced by older people a hundred years ago – a clearly absurd concept. Increases in the pension over a number of years have in fact more generally followed average earnings rather than inflation. However, because the number of pensioners has increased year by year, the actual share of national wealth received by each pensioner does not truly reflect the increase in national prosperity (see Appendix, Tables 2 and 5).

Townsend and Walker have suggested ways in which substantial pension increases can be funded without greatly upsetting the status quo,[54] and a great step forward as made when in 1975 Barbara Castle piloted the Labour government legislation for the earnings link. In 1979 this progressive measure was abolished by the Thatcher government which reinstated the price/inflation base. Once more, the gap between the basic pension and average living standards would tend to widen.

Although self-funding, the outgoings of the national insurance fund are counted as government expenditure. In pursuance of reducing this, the present government has targeted to reduce the state proportion of total national retirement income, namely state pensions, from the present 60 per cent to 40 per cent. This has focused efforts to promote personal saving schemes, private and occupational pensions, rather than upon improving the level of state pensions. However, private plans are less available to the lower paid. Moreover, private pensions and savings plans depend upon a consistently healthy financial sector and stock market. Occupational pensions also depend upon thriving, well-established employers with little risk of going into liquidation. In view of their essential private finance industry base, the government has little

---

[54] P. Townsend and A. Walker, *New Directions for Pensions–How to Revitalise National Insurance*, Pamphlet No. 2, European Labour Forum, Bertrand Russell House, Nottingham, 1995.

control over these schemes, apart from putting in place some measures to protect employees from a total loss of occupational pensions in the event of company failures. Nothing guarantees pension security as well as the state national insurance system. This was evident in the last twenty years of the twentieth century when private and occupational pension funds fell disastrously short of expectations due to falls in stock values.

Aware of the inadequacy of the basic pension, Barbara Castle was responsible for introducing the 'state earnings related pension' in 1979. This could augment the full basic pension by up to some 25 per cent of average earnings. It is now being replaced by the Second State Pension which is less favourable and excludes the lowest paid. Regrettably, the current national insurance state basic pension contributory system does not cater adequately for all women. Only 20 per cent of women receive the full pension.[55] Women who have spent years caring for others or who have been engaged in low paid or part time work, are unable to build up a full contribution record. They may have no independent entitlement to a basic pension or receive substantially less than the full amount. Many depend upon their husband's contributions. The only way to right this injustice would be to remove their obligation to contribute. National Insurance is flexible: it can accommodate such a measure as it allows for changes to both contributions, the level of pensions, and for 'crediting in' those unable to contribute. It is proven and secure and operates at low cost. Its accounts are subject to parliamentary approval.

Good health is vital in retirement, without it no amount of pension can be of benefit. The introduction of the National Health Service has for older people been perhaps the greatest blessing of the welfare state, Before the Second World War quality of treatment in illness largely depended upon personal wealth. Whilst not putting anything into their pockets, the National Health Service has provided access to the best medical treatment, regardless of income. It has removed what has always been a very serious worry of older people on small incomes, and with no back-up from employment insurance, who, were generally last in the queue... After the war, that changed. A history of paupers' progress, therefore, has to include a reference to the radical nature of the welfare state's provision

---

[55] Women's Working Party, *Wise-up on Pensions: An NPC Guide for Working Age Women*, National Pensioners Convention, London, 2005.

of free medical treatment, which has hugely improved the life of the poor and particularly poor old people.

Although as long ago as AD 131, the Greek Galen had said that diseases were caused by conditions 'contrary to nature.'[56] – and it's beyond dispute that there's nothing contrary to nature in growing old – it was commonplace to accept that old age and bad health went together. Poverty is the harbinger, not only of suffering and misery, but also of premature death. Mortality rates remain related to poverty, but we have seen that the growth of national wealth has been accompanied by an increase in the numbers who live the full lifespan. The notion that there has been an increase in the human *lifespan* is misleading, what has taken place is increasing life expectancy. History provides abundant accounts of men and women, in times gone by, who have reached a very old age, even more than a hundred. For instance, a study of 2,022 ancient Greek funerary inscriptions by B.E. Richardson, showed that one man in this group lived until he was 110.

It has been widely believed that God played a major role in deciding how long we deserve to live, we should not be surprised, therefore, that, when medical science was in its infancy, the recommended route to old age was via sobriety and a holy life. It is recorded that ages reached by bishops of France steadily increased from 52 years, in the sixteenth century to 58 in the early seventeenth century, to 66 in the late seventeenth century, and to 74 in the late eighteenth century – no doubt evidence of their growing virtues. But, there's indisputable evidence that during this period the poor and hungry generally died earlier than the rich and well fed. Most of the advice on dieting was given by those whose main problem was to resist the temptation of over-eating. Venetian Luigi Cornaro, born in Padua in 1467, wrote *Discourses on a Sober and Temperate Life* which recommended avoiding 'indulging in palate and appetite'. Having reached the age of 95, he wrote to Barbaro, Patriarch Elect of Aquileia, that he was well, melodious of voice and active. He was 98 when he died in 1565.

Some of the contemporary cures to combat illness may well have motivated medical research. For example, Dom Nicolas Alexandre hit on

---

[56] B. Livesley, *Galen, George 3rd and Geriatrics*, The Ostler Lecture of 1975, Worshipful Society of Apothecaries, London, 1975.

a remedy in the early eighteenth century for 'trembling of the head in elderly men'. He prescribed a solution of peacock dung in eau de vie to be taken on an empty stomach over three days!

How to live to a ripe old age was a great concern to the rich and powerful. In 1635 William Harvey, famous for his work on the circulation of the blood, at the request of King Charles, performed a post-mortem examination on Thomas Parr. Harvey's report has become a classic of medical history. The recorded age of Thomas Parr relied on oral evidence that also asserted that in his 127th year he was still enjoying an active sexual relationship with his wife. This was not questioned by William Harvey who reported that his organs, including his brain, and perhaps more to the point, his penis and scrotum, were in good condition. Harvey concluded that the cause of death 'seemed fairly referrible to a sudden change in non-naturals, the chief being connected with a change of air'. Winnington in County Salop where Thomas Parr was born had pure air, whereas in London, where he had been brought to live for the last 20 years of his life, 'ditches abound and filth and offal lie scattered about, to say nothing of sulphurous coal'.[57] Here was a case worthy of deeper investigation. After all, doing without the glamour of London is no great sacrifice in order to live 152 years.

Unfortunately it was not until the nineteenth-century that improvements in the environment, public hygiene and the later focus on nutrition laid the basis of a healthier nation with more of the population reaching and surpassing that magic lifespan of three score and ten (see Appendix, Tables 3 and 4).

The poor laws allowed for medical relief but the workhouse infirmary offered little more than a bed and shelter. The novels of Charles Dickens provide an insight into the plight of the ill old pauper. In the 16 September, 1865 issue of the two-penny journal, *All the Year Round* which he edited, an article appeared based upon a contemporary report in the *Lancet*. This deplored the gross neglect of the aged and sick in London workhouses. Sick-ward accommodation was only 300 cubic feet space per patient. This was actually less than the 500 cubic feet minimum ruled by the Poor Law and compared to the 1,300 to 2,000 cubic feet then being

---

[57] W. Harvey, *The Works of William Harvey*, trans. R. Willis, London, 1847.

provided by the London Voluntary Hospitals. Deaths in workhouse infirmaries were largely the result of malnutrition and neglect. These remained causes of premature death well into modern times.

In 1945 the time had arrived to seriously review the treatment of illnesses in older people, and particularly poor old people.. Dr Marjory Warren in 1936 had suggested that geriatrics should become a special branch of medicine, and in 1948 the Medical Society for the Care of the Elderly was formed, later to become the British Geriatric Society. The National Health Service Act of 1948, and the funding that it provided, enabled the medical profession to at last make a worthwhile contribution to the quality of life of older people. The days of bizarre treatments, quack and patent medicines were drawing to a close. The healthcare of the elderly fifth of the population became a major concern of the medical profession.

The National Health Service together with the national insurance based basic state pension both at the core of the welfare state, are two of the most important milestones in the nation's progress to combating deprivation in old age.

The end of the road?

We have left behind slavery and the misery of the medieval peasant, but, it remains a common perception that there will always be rich and poor. It is true that a hundred years ago Britain did not possess the technology or the economic basis to make life bearable for the underclass, especially when they were unable to work, but things have changed. Gross inequality, destitution and deprivation are no longer acceptable. The argument that harsh exploitation is needed to create capital investment for trade and industrialisation is no longer tenable. Human rights are finding their way into legislation. Now we struggle to define poverty.

Since Charles Booth talked about the 'endowment of old age', we have made considerable progress towards achieving it. The aged pauper of 1892 would find life today absolute heaven. Two factors have made this possible. The first, and most obvious, is that over the last century Britain has become wealthier. The amount available for caring for the elderly has increased – you can't get blood out of a stone! The second is that, in response to public pressure, the government has transferred more of this wealth to those in need. Destitution is no longer commonplace – but as long as older people are denied comfort and dignity in their last few years, they are in poverty.

It seems reasonable to suggest that retirement income should ensure a bit more than subsistence. Income in retirement should surely provide a warm and comfortable home, adequate clothing, and the ability to continue the sort of life enjoyed before retirement. It is hardly extreme to expect that an older person's income might allow for an annual holiday, the occasional drink with friends, a visit the cinema or, now and then, other life-enhancing treats: certainly this is unlikely to come out of the basic pension (£84.25 in 2006).

However, older citizens find it impossible to maintain the standard of living they enjoyed when working. Any hope they may have had for a comfortable, stress-free retirement will have proven to be but a dream. Already, as many as one in four have to seek means-tested income support (now known as 'minimum income guarantee' or 'pension guarantee'). The number entitled to claim is projected to more than double in the next 10 years. This is state charity and many do not claim it because they feel it demeaning to do so.

The basic retirement pension is but 16 per cent of the average wage. Consequently, the standard of living of most older people is much lower than that of the average worker. Money doesn't solve everything. It may not provide happiness but, 'rather miserable and rich than miserable and poor!' As well as financial worries, older people must contend with poor health and increasing fragility. Loneliness and bereavement add to problems that the gap in life left through the loss of a daily work regime. Difficulty in getting about makes access to leisure and participation in the community burdensome, and for millions who live alone, or even for those with an equally aged husband or wife, the possibility of needing long-term care in their declining years is a nightmare. Local authorities could do much to change this state of affairs. But the view that the aged are objects of charity prevails instead of recognising that the pensioner has not only the responsibility of contributing to the financing of local government but also the right to benefit from it's services.

Poor people have always encountered difficulties in keeping warm in winter. Cold is often the cause of premature death of the elderly. In 1849, George Day produced evidence to show that most older Londoners died during the coldest months of the year. Over the five years between 1 January 1843 and 31 December, 1847, deaths, unconnected with any obvious disease, of people of 60 years and older were 60 per cent more during December to March, than those occurring between June and September.[58] As long as the charity Help the Aged feels obliged to bring to the public attention that old people die every year due to being cold (in 2004 they numbered 31,000), it is obvious that 'fuel poverty' still exists.

---

[58] G.E. Day, MD, FRCP, A Practical Treatise on the Domestic Management & Most Important Diseases of Advanced Life, London, T.&W. Boone, 1849.

Paul Menchik of Michigan State University observed that death rates of older black and white men were related to wealth and the number of spells of poverty they experienced. The highest death rates were amongst the less wealthy. He also concluded that poorer people, on average, consequently drew less state pension than the wealthier, because fewer lived to pensionable age, and because those that did, lived fewer years to enjoy it,[59] 'to those that have more, more years shall be given!'

Townsend, and others, have shown that death rates are linked to unemployment and low income.[60] The mortality of older people is highest in those London boroughs with the most unemployment and greatest poverty. The mean crude mortality rates of residents 65 years of age and older in the 25 most depressed wards in London was 63.78 per thousand between 1982 and 1984, whereas in the 25 least deprived, the rate was 55.52. In Hackney, unemployment in 1986 was 22.7 per cent; and there, the death rate of those between 60 and 64 was over 40 per cent higher than that of the same group in the relatively wealthy borough of Bromley. In 2005 the average expectation of life of a working man in Glasgow was 11 years less than that of a male resident of Chelsea.

Some 20 per cent of the British people are now over 65 and, whilst not equalling Parr's record, happily expect to reach a good age. A long life is not for everyone, but all run the risk of fragility and the need for care during later years. If an older person has an income that's quite a bit more than average or has a family able to help, the care they require can be promptly obtained privately, and they are likely to enjoy the maximum possible comfort and dignity. Those less fortunate rely upon the modest services subsidised by the community, not always adequate, and still of an institutional nature.

In spite of the enormous benefits of the National Health Service, much has to be done to fully provide sympathetic care from cradle to grave, the basic objective of the welfare state. Older people, in long-term care, whether rich or poor, need something more dignified than a comfortable wait for the arrival of the undertaker. They should be actively involved,

---

[59] P.L. Menchik, *Economic Status as a Determinant of Mortality among Black and White Older Men: Does Poverty Kill?*, Population Studies No. 47, The Population Investigation Committee, London School of Economics, Nov. 1993.

[60] P. Townsend, P. Corrigan and U. Kowarzik, *Poverty and Labour in London*, Low Pay Unit & Poverty Research (London) Trust, 1987.

as much as possible, in managing their final years. To achieve this, a new approach to the organisation of social services and the training of social workers is required. It's not a new problem, and a scheme proposed nearly three hundred years ago could well point to a solution.

In 1727, when he was 67, Daniel Defoe, deeply disturbed by contemporary insensitive and undignified treatment of the aged, put forward a scheme for a cooperative residential home for older people. He called it the Protestant Monastery.[61] To eliminate the indignity suffered by many in their declining years he proposed that 50 old persons should form a joint stock company with a capital of £20,000. Each partner was expected to contribute £400. A house or hall in the town or country was to be rented and be divided into 20 apartments and there was to be provision for a kitchen and infirmary. A full-time paid staff would be engaged. The eventual residents would observe 'decent equality' in furnishings and hopefully in personal dress. The importance of the elderly inmates taking decisions and controlling management was stressed .

This was in marked contrast to the concept that the elderly are invariably incapable of running their affairs and have to be treated like children. Unfortunately, Defoe's scheme has never been put into practice. Anyway, it was quite out of the reach of the vast majority of older people at that time who were in poverty. However, it does imply an early appreciation of the importance of older people taking an active role in their own day-to-day care. Today, when the public purse is so much greater, it would seem feasible that many long-term care homes could adopt a measure of residents' participation in management. Older people, who now look forward to many years of active retirement, need to be included in the political life of the nation and locality. Their participation and enjoyment of theatre, music and the arts is also an essential element of defeating isolation. A lot can be done within the existing framework.

Although the spectre of destitution has been exorcised, a growing number of pensioners depend upon state benefits to make ends meet. They are officially 'poor'. Their past contribution to society means little and, unlike the working population, they will have no wage rises to

---

[61] Moreton (D. Defoe), *The Protestant Monastery*, Guildhall Library, London, 1727, Dewey 362.6, Bay H.1.4, No.15.

provide for daily needs which increase with age. What personal income is required to eradicate aged poverty? On reaching retirement would the queen's needs be met by a state pension which is less than £114 per week, the current level of Income Support? If retirement income is related to subsistence, then perhaps this or say the lowest wage currently being paid to workers would suffice. Would it be reasonable to suggest that both the queen and the elderly lady without other means would avoid being in poverty with a weekly income in the region of £150?

The European Union's objective 'of enabling people to maintain living standards' is acknowledged in the UK government's national pension strategy. It suggests that a second pension is the way this will be achieved.[62] However, present schemes are not universally accessible, any more than is the entitlement to a full state basic retirement pension.

As we enter the twenty-first century, the basic state pension approximates to only 16 per cent of the average wage but, because it is linked to inflation instead of average earnings, which rise faster, year by year this percentage steadily declines. Lord Turner's Pensions Commission Report to the government in 2005 indicates that if no action is taken on indexation, the basic pension will drop to 5 per cent of average earnings by 2060.[63] Regretably no immediate action is recommended either on this, or, on raising the current state pension. The report focuses upon sophisticated long term saving schemes which, of course, do nothing to improve the lot of the existing 11 million pensioners, or those approaching retirement. To bank on more than a very basic subsistence, it is necessary to have been able to put money under the mattress in earlier years The current basic pension with means-tested top-ups merely keeps hunger from the door,. Is this in the spirit of the welfare state?

Sir William Beveridge said that the welfare state depended upon full employment.[64] I question this. During the war, when the committee drew up their report, every able-bodied man and woman was employed on the

[62] Department of Work and Pensions, The United Kingdom National Strategy Report on the Future of Pension Systems – An update report to the Social Protection Committee on the UK's Progress since 2002, HM Government, Department of Work and Pensions, July 2005.

[63] The Stationery Office, *A New Pension Settlement for the Twenty first Century; The Second Report of the Pensions Commission*, The Stationery Office, London, 2005.

[64] Sir William Beveridge, Cd Report, *Social Insurance & Allied Services*, Parliamentary Papers, 1942–1943.

land, in the factories or in the armed forces, and most of this activity was devoted to destruction or the manufacture of weapons. In spite of this, the government was still able to take responsibility for everyone's well-being, and the poverty of the 1930s was largely eradicated. It seems reasonable to conclude, therefore, that full employment is not the only means to ensure national well-being. The lesson of the war years lies in what was achieved by people united to share responsibility for each other and work for a common objective.

If so much was achieved when only a part of the national resources and effort was directed to produce useable wealth, it is clear that in peacetime it should be possible to maintain a society that could provide a decent life or everyone – especially children and the elderly. Poverty is linked to the average standard of living and is recognised as the state of having to live on less than 60 per cent of the national median income (in 2005, £125 per week). The basic state retirement pension is less, its merely a contribution towards this amount.

National insurance is often regarded, quite incorrectly in my opinion, as a complicated system for pension provision, and it has been suggested that a 'citizen's pension' would be a simpler alternative. Here, entitlement would be based upon residence rather than the full contribution record that applies to the national insurance basic pension. Every man and woman, regardless of their married or partnership arrangements, would receive it in full. Costs would be met from general taxation supplemented in some way by employers by, or in lieu of, their current compulsory national insurance contributions. To replace the existing well-established system smoothly would be difficult. Considerable changes to existing legislation would be necessary, and it would entail making up the loss of the national insurance contribution to the National Health Service.

As we have seen, the three most significant stages in the improvement of the life of poor older people were the Poor Law of Elizabeth I, the Old Age Pension Act of 1908 and the creation of the welfare state. The right to access healthcare and income support are now established. The early pioneers of the pension movement would certainly be impressed with how much has been achieved, but in view of our wealthy consumer society they might have expected much more.

When The Revd Francis Herbert Stead formed the National Pensions Committee in 1898, his aim was to abolish pauperism by securing a pension that was little more than the cost incurred in providing shelter in the workhouse. After the first non-contributory old age pension was won in 1908, the Committee's success inspired a wider movement of parliamentary activists, trade unionists and people of goodwill to improve upon pension support and take the campaign further towards Booth's goal 'the endowment of old age'. Several years passed before the banner was taken up by pensioners themselves who created their own organisations.

The National Spinsters Pensions Association was formed in 1937 to campaign on women's pensions. A year later the National Federation of Old Age Pension Associations joined with the National Federation of Retirement Pensions Associations to form Pensioners' Voice, a serious campaigning body of pensioners which still has many branches throughout the country. Up to 1908, the trade unions had been in the forefront of the struggle for state pensions. In the years that followed, especially after the First World War, they concentrated their campaigning efforts on occupational pension plans, which were clearly necessary to supplement the very low state old age pension. It was not until 1972 that the fight for better state pensions was given prominence by the trade union and Labour movement. The British Pensioners and Trade Union Action Committee (BPTUAA) was formed. The BPTUAA is a militant association of retired trade unionists. It has several branches which still campaign today.

The National Pensioners Convention was formed in 1979, with TUC support, by Jack Jones, the former general secretary of the Transport and General Workers Union. The objective was to create nationwide awareness of the problems faced by older people and, with support from the trade unions, to press government to take action to resolve them. One and a half million pensioners are members through affiliated bodies and form the basis of the Convention. Its affiliated groups, through various committees and conferences, elect the leadership (which is voluntary) and decide on policy..

Joanna Bornat in her chapter in *The Social Policy of Old Age*[?] emphasises the important role of trade union support for the NPC's campaign for a decent state pension. However, as public concern has grown over cuts in public expenditure, many non-union and apolitical pensioner groups such as the Association of Retired Persons and Over 50, the National Assembly of Women, the Civil Servants Pensioners Association and the National Association of Retired Police Officers have affiliated to the Convention and contributed to its leadership and policy making.

The NPC organises the annual Pensioners' Parliament, when for three days pensioner delegates from all over the United Kingdom come together to debate on pensioner issues such as income, health, community care, transport and taxation. On 9 June,2005, over 2,000 delegates at the Thirteenth National Pensioners Parliament in Blackpool unanimously adopted the *Pensioners Charter*, which has since received broad national support. This states that every man and woman on reaching state pensionable age has the right to:

- a basic state pension set above the official poverty level and linked to male average earnings

- a warm and comfortable home

- free health care treatment based on clinical need and an annual comprehensive health check plus advocacy provision

- free community care and services to assist living at home

- free long long-term care

- free nationwide travel on all public and local transport

- free education and access to leisure and cultural activities

- access to goods and services without age discrimination

- active engagement and consultation on national and local issues affecting older people

- dignity, respect and fair treatment in all aspects of their lives.

Where are we now?

Since Elizabeth I, industrial technology has increased national wealth. The proportion of the population who work has decreased, but, due to modern technology, productivity has enormously increased. Computers and machines have taken over from workers especially from those in backbreaking and dead end jobs. The working week has shortened, holidays are longer and people have more time for leisure and cultural pursuits. The year on year growth of national prosperity has enabled children to stay in education longer and more older people to expect a longer retirement.

But, the state still does not guarantee its citizens incomes which enable them to enjoy that retirement. Moreover, because the state pension they receive is not related to average earnings, the gap between pensioners' living standards and the rest of society is widening. Half of those who reach retirement now face poverty and the means-test., and, unable to afford private treatment, suffer from the erosion of the welfare state's, national health and local authority care services.

The debate still centres on costs – just as it did in the nineteenth and twentieth centuries. Older people are regarded as a section of the community who, like the poor, necessitate charitable relief. Of course, the old and the poor do have something in common. With notable exceptions, the pensioner, like the pauper, does not create wealth compared to that produced by the economically active members of society, but that some of the total should redistributed for their benefit follows from the fact that today's prosperity is based upon their lifetime's work and service. This is the older generations stake in society. It is far greater than any savings they may have been able to put to one side during their earlier life

A caring and prosperous society is duty bound to provide a yield from that lifelong investment in the form of a state basic retirement pension at a level above the poverty line, without regard to any income deservedly derived from previous earnings. Charity or private businesses cannot guarantee this. It is the duty of the state to ensure it is every man and woman's right. As long as society does not accept this responsibility we still have not reached the end of the road. Indeed, we still have a long way to go.

Appendix

Table 1

National Insurance Fund Summary of Accounts (£ billions)

	1955	**1985**	**1995**	**2002**
Opening Balance	0.3	5.2	6.8	19.3
Income				
Contributions	0.6	21.2	39.8	55.4
Other receipts	0.4	2.8	4.8	3.3
Total Receipts	1.0	24.0	44.6	58.7
Expenditure				
Ret. Pensions	0.4	17.0	40.1	50.4
Other payments	*0.2	6.0	2.3	3.2
Administration Cost		0.8	1.2	0.8
Total spent	0.6	23.8	43.6	54.4
Accumulated Fund	0.3	5.4	7.8	23.6
Recommended	0.1	4.0	7.3	9.1
Useable surplus	0.2	1.4	0.5	14.5

*includes administration costs.

(Source: Annual Abstract of Statistics Central Statistical Office and Government Actuary's Quinquenial Review April 2000)

Table 2

Basic State Pension - Costs to the Nation

	*1892	**1910**	**1990**	**2000**
Population	37.7	44.9	57.4	59.8 (million)
Pensioners	1.3**	1.1 ***	10.6	10.8 (million)
Weekly Pension	£0.25	£0.25	£46.90	£67.50 (single)
Annual Cost	0.02	0.01	22.7	42.3 (£ bn)
% of G.D.P	0.16	0.5	4.1	4.5

*   Charles Booth's recommendation - not implemented
**   60+
***   70 +

Table 3

Death rates per 1,000 in different age groups (England & Wales)

	Age Males			Age Female		
Year	0-4	45-54	85 and over	0-4	45-54	85 and over
1871	71.7	20.0	312.8	62.4	15.9	290.3
1901	59.0	18.0	276.5	49.5	13.8	247.1
1931	22.4	11.6	295.9	17.4	8.3	255.3
1951	7.4	8.6	307.8	5.7	5.3	216.9
1980	3.4	6.4	230.6	2.7	3.9	188.2
2000	1.4	4.0	188.2	1.1	2.7	156.0

• United Kingdom

Sources: British Historical Statistics, B.R. Mitchell and Office for National Statistics

Table 4

Population - England and Wales (millions)

Year	1571	1671	1771	1871	1901	1931	1951	1981	2011 Projected
Total	3.271	4.983	6,448	22.71	32.537	39.95	43.76	48.52	55.15
65 plus	-	-	-	1.07	1.52	2.96	4.83	5.21	10.65

Sources: British Historical Statistics, B.R. Mitchell and Office for National Statistics

Table 5

**Ratio of Population of Working Age to Population aged 65 +
and National Wealth (annual Gross Domestic Product)**

Year	1871	1901	1931	1951	1981	2000
Ratio	19	13.3	7.7	4.4	3.2	2.8
GDP	1.0	1.6	3.8	12.6	199.4	951.0 £bn

Sources: British Historical Statistics, B.R. Mitchell and Office for National Statistics

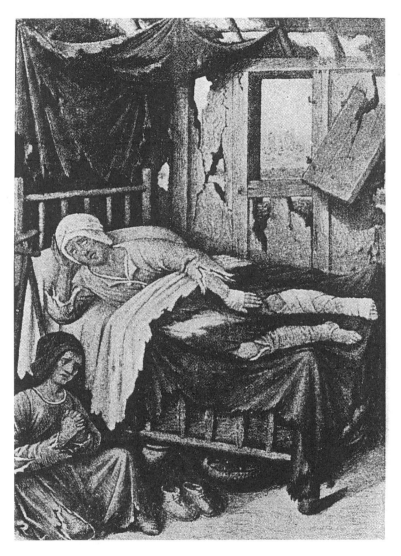

A Cottager in the 15th century

16th and 17th centuries

A rich merchant gives aims to a begger

Outdoor Relief

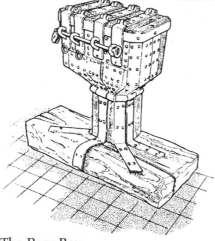

The Poor Box

Beggars' badges
Source: Journal or Archaeology V33, 1970

Rashleigh Almshouses, Cornwall, 1650 (restored 1977)

An Acte for the Releife of the Poore.

BEE it enacted by the Authoritie of this p̃sent Parliament, That the Churchwardens of everie Parish, and fower three or two substanciall Housholders there as shalbe thoughte meete, havyng respecte to the ꝓporc̃on and greatnes of the same Parishe [or·] Parishes, to be nõiated yearelie in Easter Weeke or within one monethe after Easter, under the Hande and Seale of two or more Justices of the Peace in the same Countie, whereof one to be of the Quoꝝ, dwellinge in or neere the same Parishe or Division where the same Parishe doth lie, shalbe called Overseers of the Poore of the same Parishe : And they or the greater parte of them shall take order from tyme to tyme, by and withe the consent of two or more suche Justices of Peace as is aforesaide, for settinge to worke of the Children of all suche whose Parentes shall not by the saide Churchwardens and Overseers or the greater parte of them bee thoughte able to keepe and maintaine theire Children; And alsoe for settinge to worke all such p̃sons maried or unmaried havinge no meanes to maintaine them, use no ordinarie and dailie trade of lief to get their livinge by ; and also to raise weekelie or otherwise, by Taxac̃on of eŭy Inhabitant Parson Vicar and other, and of eŭy Occupier of Landes Houses Tithes impropriate or Propriac̃ons of Tythes, Colemynes or saleable Underwoods, in the saide Parishe in such competent sūme and sūmes of Money as they shall thincke fytt, a convenient Stocke of Flaxe Hempe Wooll Threed Iron and other necessarie Ware and Stuffe to set the Poore on worke ; And alsoe competent sūmes of Money for and towardes the necessarie Releife of the lame impotente olde blinde and suche other amonge them beinge poore and not able to work, and alsoe for the puttinge out of suche Children to be Apprentices, to be gathered out of the same Parishe accordinge to the Abilitie of

Elizabeth Poor Law 1601

Workhouses built between 1835 and 1840
Source: The Workhouse, Kathryn Morrison; English Heritage

Workhouses dining hall
Source: Peter Higginbotham

Mealtime, Marylebone Workhouse, 1900
Source: Peter Higginbotham

Women's dinning room, St Pancras Workhouse
Source: Peter Higginbotham

Elderly ladies' uniform
Source: Peter Higginbotham

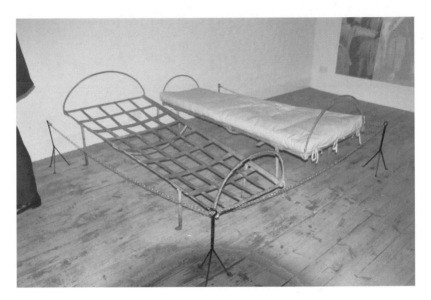

Beds in Gressenhall Workhouse
Source: Peter Higginbotham

Oakhum picking 1902
Source: PRO 30/69/1663

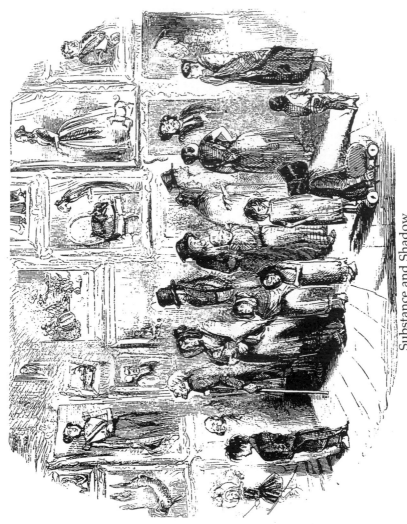

Substance and Shadow
Source: *Punch, July 15th 1843*

Francis Herbert Stead
Secretary National Pensioners Committee

Charles Booth

Edward Cadbury Treasurer,
National Pensioners Committee

Frederick Rodgers
Secretary
National Pensioners Committee

Will Crooks M.P.

Browning Hall

Clayton Hall, The conference room

This tablet is erected
in grateful commemoration of
the justice and grace of
G O D
who.when all parties in the State had left
unhelped and unhonoured
the Aged of this realm,
graciously chose to raise up in this Hall,
after exposition here on November 20th1898,
of the first Old Age Pensions Act
in the British Empire,Passed by New Zealand:
by means of the Conference held here
December 13th 1898,with
CHARLES BOOTH
in advocacy of Pensions for All in Old Age :
and by means of the
NATIONAL COMMITTEE OF ORGANIZED LABOUR
which resulted from ensuing Conferences
with Mr.Booth in Newcastle,Leeds,Manchester,
Glasgow, Bristol,and Birmingham,
A NATIONAL MOVEMENT
which,directed from this Hall,the chief officers being
Frederick Rogers, George N.Barnes,
Edward Cadbury, Francis Herbert Stead,
eventually secured as a first instalment the
OLD AGE PENSIONS ACT 1908.
thereby answering the prayers of His people
offered here and elsewhere 1898 - 1908.

Tallet erected on wall of Robert Browning Hall, Southwark

Old Age Pensions.

A

B I L L

[AS AMENDED IN COMMITTEE]

To provide for Old Age Pensions.

Ordered to be brought in by
Mr. Chancellor of the Exchequer, Mr. Asquith,
Mr. Burns, and Mr. Attorney-General.

Ordered, by The House of Commons, *to be Printed,*
1 *July* 1908.

PRINTED BY EYRE AND SPOTTISWOODE, LTD.
PRINTERS TO THE KING'S MOST EXCELLENT MAJESTY.

And to be purchased, either directly or through any Bookseller, from
WYMAN and SONS, LTD., Fetter Lane, E.C., and
32, Abingdon Street, Westminster, S.W.; or
OLIVER and BOYD, Tweeddale Court, Edinburgh; or
E. PONSONBY, 116, Grafton Street, Dublin.

[*Price* 1½*d.*]

[Bill 290.]

Old Age Pension Bill and Schedule, July 8th 1908

	Means of Pensioner.	Rate of Pension.
	Where the yearly means of the pensioner as calculated under this Act—	*s. d.*
25	Do not exceed 21*l.* - - - - -	5 0
	Exceed 21*l.*, but do not exceed 23*l.* 12*s.* 6*d.* - -	4 0
	Exceed 23*l.* 12*s.* 6*d.*, but do not exceed 26*l.* 5*s.* - -	3 0
	Exceed 26*l.* 5*s.*, but do not exceed 28*l.* 17*s.* 6*d.* - -	2 0
	Exceed 28*l.* 17*s.* 6*d.*, but do not exceed 31*l.* 10*s.* - -	1 0
30	Exceed 31*l.* 10*s.* - - - - -	No pension

Section 12: Entitlements

Pension Day 1998. Barbara Castle speaks in Trafalgar Square
On plinth: Jack Jones and Rodney Bickerstaffe

13th National Pensioners' Parliament. Blackpool June 2005

Pensioners demonstrate for the Pensioners Charter